# FINAL DESCENT

# FINAL DESCENT

## Air Crashes in Wales and the Borders

Terence R Hill

LEO COOPER

First published in 1999 by
LEO COOPER
an imprint of
Pen & Sword Books Limited
47 Church Street, Barnsley, South Yorkshire S70 2AS



**ISBN 0 85052 659 0**

A CIP catalogue of this book is available
from the British Library

Printed by Redwood Books Limited
Trowbridge, Wiltshire

*For up-to-date information on other titles produced under the Leo Cooper imprint, please telephone or write to:*

Pen & Sword Books Ltd, FREEPOST, 47 Church Street
Barnsley, South Yorkshire S70 2BR
Telephone 01226 734222

Cover painting by Rob Evans depicts Spitfire P7963 striking the barn at Lower Haughton Farm, Rednal.

# CONTENTS

# DEDICATION

This book is dedicated to all those aircrew who lost their lives in WWII, but especially to those who died during training flights over Wales and bordering counties.

I also had in mind one airman who never flew in action, or even as an aircrew member but who, nevertheless, was responsible for my interest in the RAF and aircraft in general: my late Father.

In the RNAS as a young man, he was transferred to the RAF when it was formed on 1st April 1918. As an engine fitter, he served aboard the seaplane carrier HMS Pegasus when, in 1924, the first landing by an RAF aircraft was made in Singapore. Two years later he was in South Africa, still with the same aircraft, the Fairey 111D, taking part in the historic 1926 Cape to Cairo flight – the first long distance RAF formation flight. He left the RAF soon after, but was recalled during WWII, his work at RAF Stradishall remaining the same; the engines now no longer Napier Lions but Rolls-Royce Merlins. My Father finally said goodbye to the RAF on 10th December 1945 and I joined just one week later. Between us we eventually completed forty six years service.

This book then, is dedicated also to all the unsung ground crews of the RAF both in war and peace.

**Above: Fairey IIID N9463, the first RAF aeroplane to land in Singapore 20th April 1924. My father is in the middle cockpit.**

**Below: One of the first flight of aircraft taxis back to HMS Pegasus, Singapore**

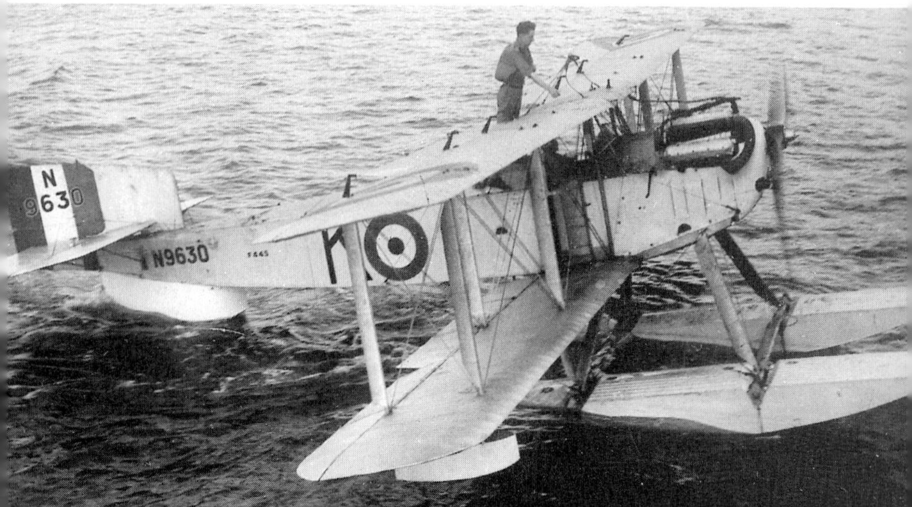

# INTRODUCTION

A number of books have been written about air crashes in Wales, including two by myself. Why another now? Many of these books were written a number of years ago and, in the intervening period, more information has come to light whilst, conversely, the physical evidence of these events has become less obvious and, in some cases, disappeared altogether. Additionally, as with all history, looking at the evidence from a different viewpoint can give the reader a greater insight into these disasters.

The main ethos of my writing has been, and still remains, the fact that I have personally visited all the sites mentioned and have not relied totally on information given to me by other researchers. The benefit of this to the reader is that everything read here will have been collected in the three years prior to publication and the sites should have changed little during this time.

**The author**
**Abingdon 1966**

Other books on the subject invariably have valuable and painstaking research included, but the photographs, sometimes over twenty five years old, frequently give a misleading idea of what the searcher might expect to find today.

Finding actual fragments has, to me, been most important. I rarely want to keep these pieces but without seeing them on site I cannot be sure that I am, indeed, at the correct location.

Sometimes, nothing whatsoever can be found and, unless I have firm documentary or other evidence, the map reference I give will be followed by an asterisk. This means that, although I have made thorough and often frequent visits to the site, no trace remains. Should, for instance, the gorse be later burnt down, or trees felled, something may, of course, yet come to light. Despite access to official documents, locations and names of crew members can still be in doubt. Take the case of Wellington L4230, which crash-landed on Great Rhos; the books I have read on the subject give the name of the pilot as one who, according to the MoD, did not exist. Have official records been mislaid, or has an incorrect name been passed down by various authors?

I myself have not been immune to such errors. In my first book I recorded the crash of a Republic P47 Thunderbolt in North Wales, giving the name of the pilot as Lieutenant Barratt. This name had been mentioned to me by several people and appeared in other books. Only after publication did I receive, from a friend in Welshpool, a copy of the USAAF official report giving the correct name as Lieutenant Beauchamp. So those in glasshouses should, I suppose, be reasonably certain of their aim before hurling missiles! Perhaps it is just as well; if any book could be totally researched to its final conclusion, not only would the cost be prohibitive but, by the time it reached publication, the sites would probably be bare and valuable records lost.

Be assured that I have taken all reasonable steps in ensuring that any information contained herein is as accurate as I can make it. Finally, although 27 crash sites are described in this book it is not, of course, a complete record. Unfortunately, many hundreds of aircraft met their end in the Principality.

* * * * *

## NOTES ON SITE FINDING

Long gone are the days when large amounts of wreckage can be found at most sites. Those in the mountains and less accessible areas naturally have the most, but this book does not venture into the highest regions. Many sites are, indeed, on level fields. The reader must be aware that permission from the landowner must be sought before proceeding; even if a marked footpath passes through a farm it is common courtesy to ask permission to use it.

It is still not unusual, fifty or so years after the event, to find witnesses to the crash, or rather those who have seen the wreckage. People who have actually seen the aircraft fall to earth are very few and far between, and the intervening years have invariably caused these memories to become distorted.

On finding a site it is a natural impulse to want to take some fragments away with you. If you must, make it just a tiny piece. It serves no purpose to remove wreckage wholesale or even to just throw it into a hedge. Put it back where it was found; far better to make a photographic record of what you discover.

Even if you are not an aircraft enthusiast, these sites can give purpose to walks in Wales and the bordering counties. Unlike golf, which someone described as a good walk spoiled, a crash site visit might be called a good walk made even better!

## AIRCRAFT WRECKAGE

The ownership of the remains of British, United States and German aircraft is vested in the Ministry of Defence.

Permission of that Ministry should be sought if it is intended to recover any parts found. This is mainly intended for groups who wish to actually excavate the site, and not really aimed at someone casually picking up a small item, however, technically, no part should be removed. This may seem a trifle ridiculous when it is known that groups, local councils, and individuals have been carting away wreckage wholesale for years, and in some cases selling it.

Really, it is best not to remove parts but to photograph them for later identification; this will also have the advantage of leaving something for successive generations to find.

The contact address for those who wish to recover items is: Ministry of Defence, Room F63, Building 255, RAF Innsworth, Gloucester GL3 1EZ

## MAPS

All references given in this book are for Ordnance Survey Landranger 1:50,000 Series (1¼ inches to the mile), although often Outdoor Leisure Maps 1:25,000 Series will prove useful

## PREFIXES and STAMPS

Nearly all parts of an aircraft have makers part numbers stamped into them (rather like cars today). In addition, production line inspectors add their own imprint. In modern aircraft these are usually stencilled, in order to avoid weakening the material.

If a part is marked with an RAF section and reference number eg 5A/1151, this means that the item is not part of the aircraft structure but can be used in a number of types, for instance, a compass. This also applies to nuts and bolts etc, which are often marked AGS (Aircraft General Standard), applicable to a number of types. Most manufacturers also prefix their part numbers with the Type model number, eg Spitfire '300'.

As well as the manufacturers' inspectors, officials of the Aeronautical Inspection Directorate (AID) often stamped major components. Below is a list of manufacturers' prefixes and component stamps applicable to some aircraft mentioned in this book. It must be remembered that, because of sub-contracting etc some may bear different marks or, indeed, no marks at all.

| Component prefixes: | Inspectors' stamps: |
|---|---|
| Wellington 285 | Airspeed AS |
| Lancaster 683 | Avro R3 |
| Spitfire 300 | Bristol FB |
| Harvard 66 | de Havilland DH |
| Anson 652A | Miles PPA |

**Above: Type 300 Spitfire**
**Left: Type 683 Lancaster**
**Below: Typical Wellington Geodetic**

**Above: Hunter showing modern stencil marking.**

**Right: Anson; many numbers but no type number evident on this piece.**

**Below: American F-111 piece with stencilled figures.**

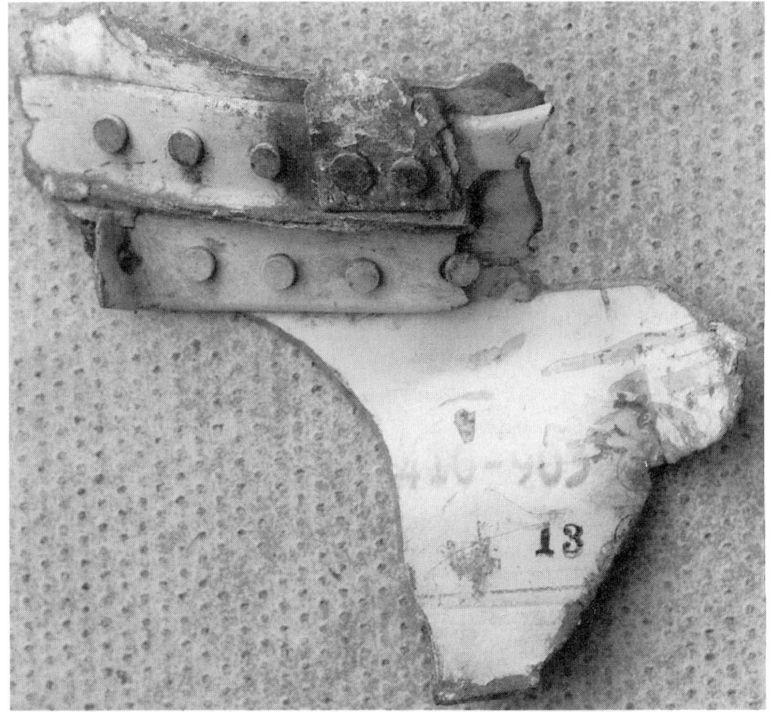

Llandudno
Rhyl
Colwyn Bay
Beaumaris
Bangor
WIRRAL
Halkyn Mtn
VALE OF CONWAY
VALE OF CLWYD
Mynydd Hiraethog
Bettws-y-coed
Snowdon
Blaenau Ffestiniog
PASS OF ABERGLASLYN
A5
A55
A548
Llangollen
VALE OF LLANGOLLEN
Criccieth
Arenig Fawr
2800
Rhinog Fawr
A487
Dolgellau
Barmouth
Shrewsbury
A458
Welshpool
Long Mtn
DOVEY VALLEY
Towyn
VALE OF POWIS
Newtown
2468
Aberystwyth
A44
1920
Rhyddhywel
CLUN FOREST
1796
Beacon Hill
1183
Mynydd Bach
North Wales Sector
1. Botha L6318 p.16
2. Anson N5154 p.21
3. Lancaster R5736 p.26
4. Vampire VZ874 p.33
5. Wellington HF519 p.38
6. Wellington BJ700 p.43
7. Oxford N4568 p.48
8. Anson N5130 p.53
Eastern Wales & Borders Sector
9. Spitfire TE210 p.57
10. Beaufighter NE203 p.60
11. Blenheim L4873 p.66
12. B17E 41-9098 p.70
13. Washington WF502 p.76
14. Vampire 334 p.84
15. Baltimore AG689 p.90
16. Audax K7435 p.101
17. Spitfire P7963 p.107
18. Spitfire P7280 p.112
19. Anson K6248 p.118
Llanbedr & Dolgellau Sector
20. Wellington HX433 p.122
21. Wellington HE872 p.126
22. Wellington N2866 p.131
Mid Wales Sector
23. Wellington L4230 p.136
24. Martinet HN888 p.140
25. Harvard N7077 p.143
26. Hunter XE680 p.147
27. Hunter XJ637 p.151

## THE COUNTRY CODE

1. RESPECT THE LIFE AND WORK OF THE COUNTRYSIDE
2. GUARD AGAINST ALL RISK OF FIRE
3. LEAVE GATES AS YOU FIND THEM
4. KEEP DOGS UNDER CONTROL
5. KEEP TO PUBLIC PATHS ACROSS FARM LAND
6. TAKE YOUR LITTER HOME
7. PROTECT WILDLIFE, PLANTS and TREES
8. TAKE CARE ON COUNTRY ROADS
9. HELP KEEP WATER CLEAN
10. DON'T DAMAGE TREES, HEDGES and WALLS

# North Wales

***Botha L6318, No.3 School of Gunnery and Reconnaissance, on a navigational training flight from Squires Gate, crashed 23 August 1942 on Tal-y-Fan.***

**Crash site map number 1** **Map reference 115/740736**

Built at the Blackburn works at Brough,Yorks, the Botha was designed to Air Ministry specification M 15/35 (as was the more successful Bristol Beaufort) as a general reconnaissance and torpedo bomber. The prototype L6104 made it's first flight on 28th December 1938. With two Bristol Perseus radial engines of 880 hp it was woefully underpowered and with other shortcomings it was only allocated to two squadrons: Numbers 502 and 608.

**A Botha during ground engine run. Note the open crew door on starboard side and bomb rack under wing.**

Despite this, 580 Bothas were built and these were used by OTUs as bombing, gunnery and radio trainers where, without the necessity of carrying a full bomb load over any great distance, were able to perform these duties adequately. Having an engine failure in a Botha just after take-off when fully laden, must have been interesting, to say the least.

The Botha was officially declared obsolete in August 1943 although a few continued in service until September 1944.

On 23rd August 1942, L6318 took-off from No.3 School of Gunnery and Reconnaissance, Squires Gate near Blackpool on a navigational training flight. The crew were:

SGT. H. L. PENDAL Pilot
SGT. R. W. PATRICK Nav/BombAimer
SGT. J. B. WOOD (RNZAF) Nav/BombAimer
ACI A. SMYTHE Air Gunner
ACI R. IBBOTSON Air Gunner

There was thinnish cloud over North Wales at about 1500 feet. L6318 entering this, whilst over the coast flew into the extreme eastern end of Tal-y-Fan, killing all those on board. A trained observer is said to have seen the aircraft's pitot head, (the pitot head supplies outside air to the Airspeed Indicator) with the cover still on, at the site. If this was the case, the pilot may have had no indication of the speed of the aircraft and it could have stalled, failing to recover before hitting the ground.Why did the aircraft leave Squires Gate with a faulty ASI, instead of landing immediately? This is one question which will unfortunately, never be answered.

The starting place for this walk is Llangelynin Church at

**Llangelynin Church is a good place to begin your walk to the crash site on Tal-y-Fan.**

**The crash site with Conwy in the far distance.**

Garnedd-wen. As the walk. including search, only takes about two hours or so, the opportunity should not be missed to explore the area more fully. A good starting place is the church itself.

Go over the stile to reach this remote little church, restoration of which was made possible by the late Gerald Speechley. The main fabric of the building is from the 14th century and the oak timbers. especially over the porch, are noteworthy. Most of the gravestones are from the 18th century.

The whole area is surrounded by a thick stone wall of irregular shape having only one gate which is not visible on the approach. You are left to guess which way will lead to the gate and which will come to a dead end! (I chose the latter).

A half mile or so past the crash site are the remains of a quarry, now disused, which is the nesting place of the comparatively rare Ring 0usel.

Nearby stand stone remains of a Peat house, found only in this part of Wales. While ancient Standing Stones and the site of the Caer Bach iron-age fort are also in the area.

In case the reader thinks that he has opened a local history book by mistake, I will get to the main object of the walk.

After passing the No Vehicles sign, turn right walking up hill, through a very muddy gateway, cross the field to where two stone walks pinch in together and a small stream runs between them.

A few hundred yards further on, and before getting to a ruined building on the right. look for a wall going uphill on the left. This is not quite as easy as it sounds as the whole area is criss-crossed by stone walls. mostly in a very good state of preservation. About 300 yards uphill alongside the wall is a very wet patch of ground. A central stream, or more accurately, a rivulet, of water issues from under the wall and meanders downhill. This is the crash site. Only tiny remains can be found and these in the stream itself, which is so small that heather often covers it completely.

When I was last there, a friendly farmer with his three dogs approached and we chatted about the area. He had no recollection at all of the crash remembering only that the land around us had been used for Army training area during the war. He was able to help though by telling me that this was the only place where the stream came out from under the wall.

Don't be misled by the spent cartridge cases that abound in

the area, or the 2 inch mortar bomb fins. These are evidence of army training, and not of the crash site.

Sometimes the business end of a mortar bomb can be found. They are probably inert, but I do not know; sheep have trampled them for years to no effect, but my advice is, as for other types of ammunition: don't take a chance, leave them alone.

**The Botha, overweight and underpowered – Blackburn's attempt to produce a maritime search aircraft.**

***Anson N5154, No.11 Advanced Flying Unit, on a navigational training flight from Shawbury, crashed 16th February 1943 at Nant Mawr farm.***

**Crash site map number 2** **Map reference 116/894696**

The Anson was affectionately known as 'Faithful Annie' to those who came into contact with 'her' and most aircrew did, at one time or another. After a brief period on operations, at the beginning of the war, it was replaced by more suitable types and began a new career as an aircrew trainer. Powered by two Armstrong-Siddeley Cheetah IX radial engines, of 350 hp each, it cruised at a sedate 158 mph. This was quite enough for the trainee navigators twiddling their calculators and sweating over the problems of dead-reckoning, map reading and wind velocities. Unfortunately, many of these would-be navigators lost their bearings, so that the mountains and hills of Britain took a heavy toll of lives as aircraft descended through cloud over what was thought to be lower ground.

Although 11 (P)AFU was a pilots' training unit, this appears to have been a navigational exercise, perhaps explained by the fact that navigators were also trained at Shawbury. One of a batch of five hundred, Anson N5154 was built at an A V Roe factory in Manchester. (It is interesting to note that the next aircraft on the line, N5155, was delivered to the Royal Hellenic Air Force.) The Anson's Cheetah engines were serial numbered 177763 and 177779 and it was these engines, showing a marked

**A trainee navigator plots his course in the 'greenhouse'.**

reluctance to run in the damp February air, which were the cause of this particular crash. Fortunately, on this occasion, no lives were lost.

At 1345 hours on 16th February 1943, N5154, piloted by Flying Officer D L Sedgwick, took off for a cross-country flight during which the trainee navigator would plot courses to a number of turning points. As a staff pilot, Flying Officer Sedgwick, with three hundred and seventy seven flying hours to his credit, was a mere 'bus driver', allowing his trainee charges to exercise their new found skills in navigation. However, it was the pilot's skills which were soon to be tested and not found wanting.

Forty minutes later, flying down the Elwy valley in the base of cloud with a high icing index, the main jets in the carburettors iced up; the slow running jets remaining clear. The engine revolutions dropped down to tick-over speed and the exercise changed from one of navigation to the urgent selection of a field suitable for a forced landing.

Making a normal landing with the undercarriage down would, most likely, have caused the aircraft to nose over and winding the wheels down by hand in such a short time was, in any case, probably not an option. In any event, Flying Officer Sedgwick elected for a wheels-up belly landing. Spotting a field near the river at Nant Mawr, he made an approach from the north, clipping the tree tops at the end of the field. The aircraft, skidding across the field, came to rest in a muddy ditch with its nose and engines protruding through the far hedge.

No doubt breathing a collective sigh of relief, the crew evacuated the aircraft. They were met by a small boy, running down from Nant Mawr farm and later joined by another lad from the farm across the way.

Soon the emergency services were on the scene. (Well, at least the local policeman appeared and made appropriate notes in his little book.) Transport was provided for the crew, who were taken to the Stag Inn at Llangernyw. Here they awaited transport back to Shawbury, refreshing themselves in the meantime, no doubt, with the hospitality of the house.

The subsequent Court of Inquiry decided that the pilot was in no way to blame and the file was quickly put away.

* * * * *

Whilst looking for the sites of other crashes in the Llangernyw area, I contacted the ex-Mayor of Colwyn Bay, Mr John Hughes. Not only did he know of the sites I was seeking but mentioned this Anson, not previously known to me and agreed to accompany me to investigate.

Together with the small boy from Nant Mawr farm and his companion from nearby Bryn Gwynlan, both now fifty four years older of course, we met at the crash site. The gap in the hedge made by the crashing aircraft remains, though the ditch has since been filled in. Mr Williams, the boy from Nant Mawr farm, told me that the pilot's face was covered with muddy ditchwater which the RAF man mistakenly thought was blood!

The Wireless operator survived the war and now lives,

John Hughes, left, and Idwal Vaughan from Bryn Gwynlan, return to the gap in the hedge made by the crashing Anson over fifty years ago.

The Stag hotel Llangernyw where Flying Officer Sedgwick and his crew were taken after the crash of N5154.

apparently, on the Lancashire coast. Some years ago he came to visit the site, whilst on holiday in the area but, unfortunately, his name and address have been mislaid.

Locating a site which is not mentioned in other reference books and, more particularly, where the aircraft number is not known, is not always easy. In this case, however, the Library and Information Services of Flintshire County Council came to the rescue by putting me in touch with the archives where Police records are stored. No – the bobbies' little black books are not kept but the station records are. These baldly stated that an Anson aeroplane, number N5154, crash-landed near Nant Mawr farm, with no casualties. With the co-operation of Anna McIlwaine, of the RAF Museum, the rest was easy.

REMINISCENCES

My own experience of the Anson was limited to two flights as a passenger. One, in midwinter from Evanton Scotland, to Hendon, the other in midsummer from Fayid Egypt, to Aquaba Jordan.

The first trip saw me freezing for four hours in the draughty cabin. I recall the hunched figure of the Warrant Officer pilot, raincoat collar turned up against the cold, a packet of Capstan Full Strength propped up on the instrument panel and an expression on his face clearly indicating his desire to be elsewhere.

On the second I found myself similarly seated but sweltering hot and with the Station Commander as pilot, on the approach to Aquaba with the warning horn blaring to remind him that he had forgotten to lower the undercarriage!

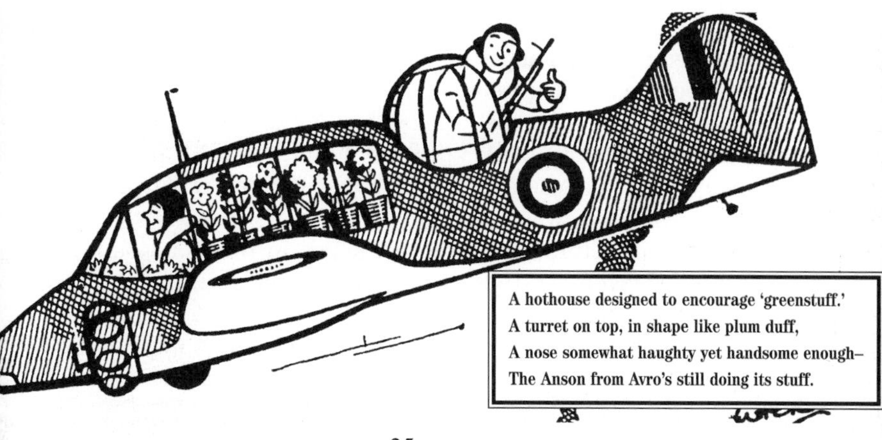

**A hothouse designed to encourage 'greenstuff.'**
**A turret on top, in shape like plum duff,**
**A nose somewhat haughty yet handsome enough–**
**The Anson from Avro's still doing its stuff.**

***Lancaster B Mk1 R5736, 1660 Conversion Unit, on a night navigational exercise from Swinderby, crashed 6th July, 1943 near Llangernyw.***

**Crash site map number 3** **Map reference 116/862676**

The Lancaster was designed at the A V Roe factory by Roy Chadwick, another of whose aircraft, the Anson, also appears in these pages. The Lancaster's predecessor, the Manchester, was not a success, mainly due to its twin power plants. These were the new Rolls-Royce Vulture 24 cylinder in-line engines of 1760 hp; insufficient development meant that they were, however, not only unreliable but unable to produce the designed power output.

Although more than just a four-engined version of the Manchester, the Lancaster used many of its predecessor's components and needed comparatively little redesign. It was, as is well-known, the most successful of the three British four engined bombers of WWII and was produced in greater numbers: the Lancaster 7377, Halifax 6176 and Stirling 2221.

The Stirling was compromised in its design by non-operational factors and, although active in Bomber Command until 8th September 1944, was gradually replaced by the other types.

The Halifax too had its share of problems and it was not until the Mark III version appeared that its full potential was realised.

The Lancaster was right first time. Although a number of variants appeared, it was a Mark 1 which was the last to enter RAF service on 2nd February 1946. Judged to be the most successful British bomber it was still not able to defend itself in daylight.

Its existence was first made public after the daring daylight attack on the MAN diesel works at Augsburg, on 17th April 1942. Sqn Ldr J D Nettleton later received the VC for his leadership in this heroic action (the first of ten recipients of this award whilst flying Lancasters) but, of the twelve aircraft taking part, only five returned home.

In the night bomber role, the Lancaster's part in Nazi Germany's downfall was crucial, dropping over 608,000 tons of bombs. Most aircraft used at OTUs and HCUs were, as the Americans aptly put it, 'War-weary'; used extensively on operations, they had been replaced by newer machines. They were not unsafe or defective but, relieved of the requirement to

**Lancaster cockpit.**

transport full bomb loads over long ranges, were perfectly adequate for training.

With the first Lancaster operations taking place in early 1942, Bomber Command embarked on an extensive training programme. As there were few, if any, 'weary' Lancasters around new aircraft that had not seen operational service were used; R5736 was one of these.

Starting life at A V Roe's factory at Manchester, as part of contract number B69274/40, R5736 was allocated, on 12th July 1942, to number 50 squadron at Skellingthorpe, Lincolnshire. The next day it was re-allocated to 1654 Conversion Unit then, after a month, to 207 Conversion Flight and finally, on the last day of 1942, to 1660 CU at Swinderby. (The term Heavy Conversion Unit does not seem to have been used at this time.) R5736 survived for another six months before it was lost with its crew of six.

* * * * *

Sgt E A Orchard had two hundred and forty three solo flying hours to his credit, some on the Manchester, but only four hours in Lancasters.

On 6th July 1943 Sgt Orchard and his crew were briefed for a night navigational exercise. In view of indifferent weather conditions, stress was placed on maintaining safety height, especially over the mountains of Wales.

During the flight the navigator believed they had crossed over

**Wireless operator's position in a Lancaster.**

**The crash site is now overgrown with Rhododendrons.**

**Mr L Roberts and the Lancaster tail wheel strut.**

high ground but must have asked the pilot for a visual fix. The aircraft descended into a gloom of thickening cloud and lashing rain. Depending on his altimeter setting, the pilot must have realised, with some concern, that they were down to about 1000 feet but still unable to see the ground; tension amongst the crew must have been almost palpable. Minutes later the aircraft struck the hillside at about 700 feet, exploding on impact. Such was the force of the explosion that the engines were smashed to pieces, while other fragments were blown some distance away. The AOC agreed with the subsequent Court of Inquiry's conclusion that this crash was caused by 'an error of captaincy'.

* * * * *

The River Elwy rises in the hills near Moel Derwydd, above Pentrefoelas and meanders down the valley meeting the Afon Clwyd near St Asaph.

**Checking Rolls Royce Merlins of a Lancaster.**

**Merlin valves and part of cockpit or turret frame, including fragments of perspex.**

It is a lush valley, with green meadows and woods. Low hills undulate on either side while only two villages are found along it's 16 mile length. There are sites of four wartime air crashes in the area, all of which are featured in these pages. In two of the crashes all crew members survived but, unfortunately, twelve men died in the other accidents.

I had no map reference to guide to the site of R5736 but John Hughes, who had shown me the position of Anson N5154, remembered the location well. He told me that he helped the Mountain Rescue Team from Llandwrog (on its first call-out since it's re-organisation) in collecting fragments of bodies from the site. The work was temporarily halted when it was thought that a crew member may have escaped by parachute. A large white canvas cross was placed in the field as a marker for an aircraft, which made a search of the valley, but no sign of a parachute was seen.

The search was continued until all human remains had been collected and the salvage party arrived to remove the wreckage. Some time afterwards someone found the tail wheel oleo leg and presented it to Mr L Roberts of Moelfre where it is still propped up against a wall of his petrol station.

**Bomb Beam Guide. Ploughed up by farmer and later identified by the Engineering Officer of the Battle of Britain Flight.**

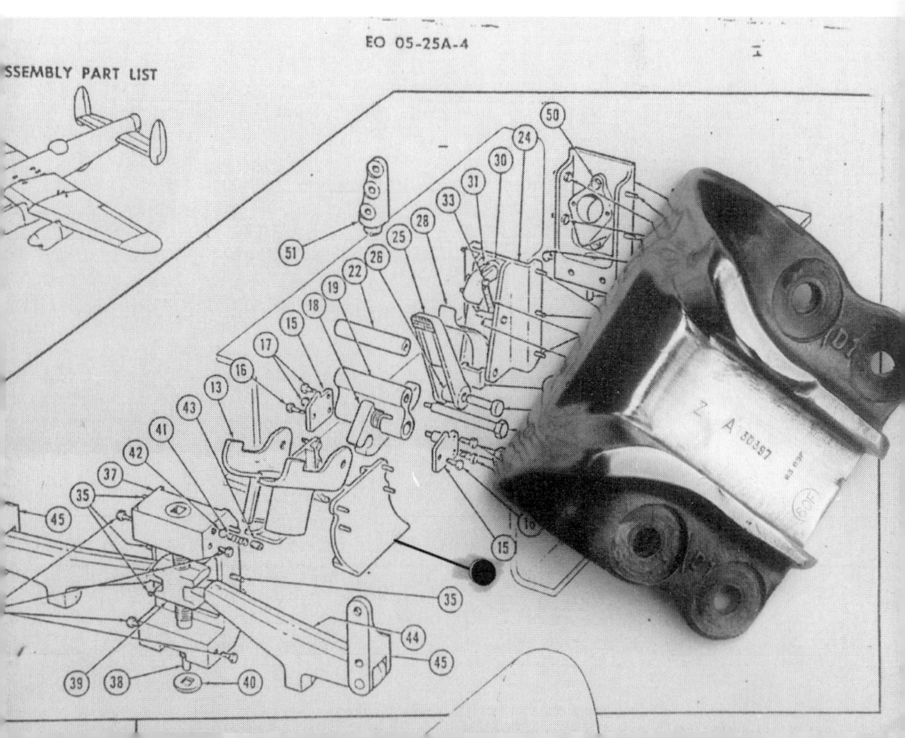

Before searching we had gained permission from the owner, as the site lies on a large estate. Mrs Mackeson-Sandbach received us graciously in her elegant old house and informed us that she clearly recalled the crash. She directed us to her farm manager who remembered ploughing up a piece of metal some years ago – and no, he hadn't thrown it away. The piece, when produced, contained a part number which enabled the Engineering Officer of the RAF Battle of Britain Memorial Flight to positively identify. It was in fact a guide for the bomb carrier which, along with the bomb, used to be winched up into the aircraft's bomb bay. I was led to the site where, with the aid of a metal detector, I was able to locate various parts including two Merlin engine valves, complete with springs and valve seats.

It must be emphasised that the location of this crash site should only be visited with the express permission of the landowner.

***Vampire FB5 VZ874, No.7 Flying Training School, on night flying and circuits from Valley, crashed 12th October, 1956 on Mynydd Mawr.***

**Crash site map number 4** **Map reference 115/539547 (impact) 545546 (debris)**

The only Allied jet fighter to see service in WWII was the Gloster Meteor. On the drawing board some months later, the Vampire first flew on 20th September 1943 but did not enter service, with 247 squadron, until April 1946, some time after the end of hostilities.

As in the Meteor, the jet engine used was of the centrifugal flow type designed, in this case, by Major Frank Halford. This was a development of Air Commodore Frank Whittle's original concept and had the combustion chambers arranged around the outside of the engine casing. Though certainly efficient, it did not have the development potential of the now preferred, axial flow type.

Although having metal wings, the fuselage of the Vampire carried on in the tradition of its forbear, the Mosquito, in being built of a plywood and balsa sandwich. Moulded in two halves,

**Mynydd Mawr from Snowdon. VZ874 crashed near the highest point of the mountain.**

the body was glued together, covered in fabric, doped and finally painted to keep out the elements.

By the time the Vampire entered service the original Halford engine design had been refined into the 'Goblin' by de Havillands, thus making it one of the few modern aircraft where both engine and airframe came from the same manufacturer.

Serving at first as a fighter, the Vampire was succeeded in 1951 by the better performing Meteor F8, whereupon it took on the new role of fighter-bomber, the FB5, which became the most widely used of all Vampires. Powered by a DH Goblin 2 of 3100 lbs thrust, the FB5 could attain 535 mph and a range of 1220 miles. Armament consisted of four 20 mm cannon and it could carry bombs or rockets under the wings. At one time or another, it formed the equipment of some thirty nine squadrons, many serving in Germany.

Widely exported to over twenty countries, the Vampire was built at the DH works at Hatfield and Broughton, also sub-contracted to Fairey Aviation and English Electric at Preston. By 1956 the Vampire had been replaced in front-line service but many continued to serve as advanced and operational trainers.

Approximately nine hundred FB5s were produced, VZ874 being a Broughton-built machine.

Valley, in Anglesey, has been an RAF training establishment for many years and, in 1951, No 7 FTS was part of No 25 Group Flying Training Command. By the time pilots reach Valley they are at an advanced stage of training and many exercises are flown solo.

Sub Lt R Davies, a Fleet Air Arm pilot undergoing this training had two hundred and thirty seven flying hours to his credit, including sixty eight dual and forty two solo on the Vampire. Having now come to the night flying phase of the course he had received four hours dual instruction and completed two hours solo. He had already flown eleven hours on instruments, with a further twenty one simulated. He had, therefore, little experience of night flying in the Vampire.

At 1910 hours, on 12th October 1956, Sub Lt Davies took off in Vampire VZ874 for local night flying and circuits. The flight took place under IFR (Instrument Flight Rules), ie cloudy conditions. Just ten minutes later, the aircraft slammed into the side of Mynydd Mawr, near the 2290 foot summit, killing the pilot instantly.

Reading the official reports of these accidents one is often struck by the insensitive tone found in the Courts of Inquiry summaries. Of course, they are enquiring into a serious occurrence and, if someone is at fault, they must not hesitate to say so, but I think there could sometimes be more subtle ways of reporting the conclusions.

In case it is I who am too sensitive, I will quote the shortened version of the summary as found on the Form 1180 verbatim in this particular instance so that the reader may judge for himself:

> *'In the opinion of the Court the pilot must bear full responsibility for the accident. They considered that the primary cause was pilot error in navigation during instrument flying, although disobedience of briefing instructions cannot be ruled out entirely.'*

I wonder if that last bit was really necessary?

**Remains of VZ874 on Mynydd Mawr. In foreground is the engine impeller.**

Although the aircraft struck the mountain near the summit, wreckage has fallen down Mynydd Mawr's eastern side and debris, including the impeller wheel, can be seen on the lower slopes.

A footpath leads up to the edge of Beddgelert Forest and continues up towards the site. There is also a privately owned track which runs from Drws-y-coed directly to the forest but this should not be used without gaining permission from the farm.

It is interesting to note that another de Havilland aircraft, Mosquito W4088, crashed only about five hundred yards away some twelve years earlier.

**De Havilland Goblin centrifugal flow jet engine.**

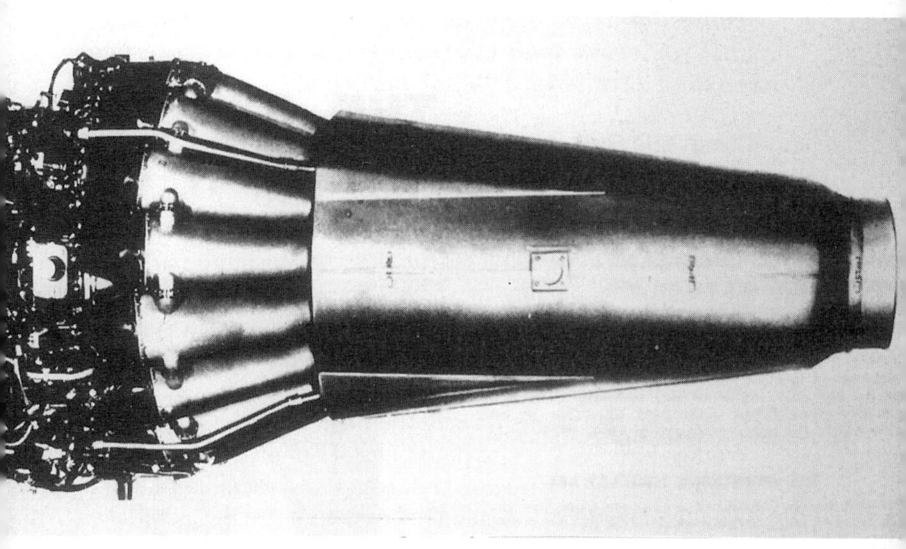

***Wellington B MX HF519, No.26 Operational Training Unit, on cross country training flight from Waterbeach, crashed 15th May, 1944 at Llanrwst.***

**Crash site map number 5** **Map reference 116/814633**

Perhaps the most remarkable aspect of the Vickers-Armstrongs Wellington in service was its versatility (often born of necessity), although it is true that the Mosquito ran it close in the multiplicity of roles in which it was used. Almost the only use to which the 'Wimpy' was not put was, perhaps not surprisingly, that of fighter. (Although the T Mk XVll played its part in radar training for night fighter crews.)

Bomber operations formed the main part of its duties but the 'Wimpy' also made its mark in Coastal Command as a mine layer, an airborne mine detector and, using a retractable search light, as an illuminator of surfaced U-boats at night. It was widely used by overseas commands and for photographic reconnaissance. Pressed into service as a trials aircraft for the Dam Busters' bouncing bombs, the 'Wimpy' was also used as a Transport and, finally, became a training aircraft.

All these duties required modifications and changes to the

basic airframe, so each model was given a Mark number for identification. The last wartime variant was the T Mk XVlll. It was, however, the earlier B Mk X (of which 3,804 were built) which continued in production until the end of the war, the last being delivered to the RAF on 13th October 1945.

After further modifications, which included removing the gun turrets, the Wellington continued (as the T10 and later T19) as a navigational trainer until replaced, in 1953, by the Valetta, also designed by Vickers. With regards to the numbering system – aircraft Mark numbers were expressed in Roman numerals until near the end of the war; from then on the Arabic form was used.

The B Mk X was, the last of the true bomber versions but, by late 1943, the Main Force of Bomber Command had been largely re-equipped with four-engined aircraft. The Wellington continued to serve in other operational commands and especially at OTUs where, at one time, twenty five units were so equipped. It was powered by two Bristol Hercules XVl radial engines, each giving 1615 hp at 2900 rpm. In an age when most aircraft use jet engines, it is interesting to note that these large piston engines each had a displacement of over 38 litres. The Hercules engines gave the Wellington a maximum speed of 255 mph at an All-up-Weight of 36,000 lbs.

**A 4000 lb bomb is loaded onto a Wellington at 21 Operational Training Unit.**

**The crash site where fragments litter the surrounding hedges.**

**A piece of HF519 found in the hedge at the crash site.**

Built at the Vickers factory at Broughton, HF519 was one of a batch of 1,100 aircraft of various mark numbers.

Flying Officer A A Tilton, a Canadian, had accrued a total of one hundred and sixty one hours solo flying by day and a further thirty four at night. Of these, thirty nine and fourteen respectively were on the Wellington.

On the afternoon of 15th May 1944 Flying Officer Tilton, his four other crew members plus a Wing screen instructor, were briefed for a cross-country flight at 10,000 feet and over. They would use 'Gee', a navigational aid, to make a simulated attack on an infra-red target before returning to their base at Waterbeach. An infra-red target was located on the ground, usually on a bombing range, though one was actually on the top of Blackpool Tower! When it was calculated that the aircraft was over the target, the bomb release was pressed and later, on return to base, study of the exposed film would show the accuracy of the attack. No actual bombs were dropped. (Fortunately for Blackpool).

The aircraft took off at 2240 hours and proceeded with the exercise as planned. 'Gee' fixes were often difficult to obtain in the Cardigan Bay area and the plots received appeared to be questionable. After two hours and twenty minutes flying the pilot, believing the information to be accurate in placing them over the sea, decided to descend to obtain a visual fix.

They broke through the cloud at 2,000 feet, over the Elwy Valley near Llanrwst. Seeing the high ground nearby, the pilot pulled back on the control column, the aircraft climbed steeply, stalled and plunged into the ground, burning fiercely. All those on board died instantly.

The Investigation and Court of Inquiry which followed were unanimous in their conclusions:

On receipt of 'Gee' bearings, believed to be corrupt, the Wireless Operator should have checked the position with the Navigator. It was the responsibility of the Wing Instructor to monitor all events as they unfolded and to advise accordingly. The pilot seemed unaware that he was not on course.

The Air Officer Commanding placed the blame squarely on the W/Op and the Wing Screen.

The accident report also stated that, with eight tenths cloud at 2,000 feet, the pilot could not have cleared the ground in any case. Study of the relevant OS map does not seem to bear out this assumption, with no ground above about 1,500 feet in the vicinity. It is likely, therefore, that the cloud base was below that reported. After the accident the minimum height for attacking infra-red targets was raised to 5,000 feet.

It is easy, after fifty years, to wonder how such basic errors could be made. Imagine for a moment, however, the dark, cloudy skies of wartime Britain; no lights to be seen, the aircraft bucking around in the turbulent air, instruments, perhaps, giving faulty readings and the Screen probably spending most of his time up front with the pilot. Perhaps now the situation doesn't look quite so straightforward after all.

Enquiries in the valley lead me to Gwyn Evans. The aircraft crashed in an adjacent farm to his which he now uses for grazing. He was therefore able to give me exact directions.

The proximity to the road must have made clearance of the wreckage a simple matter both at the time of the crash and for interested parties since. It is remarkable that anything remains at all but, just a few yards from the farm track, a crater still marks the site and the hedge is littered with small fragments.

Let us hope that these will remain as a memorial to the six airmen who died there.

**Bristol Hercules engine – the power plant for the majority of Wellingtons produced.**

***Wellington BJ700, 425 Squadron, on a navigational exercise from Dishforth, crashed 23rd September 1942 at Rhos-y-Mawn farm.***

**Crash site map number 6** **Map reference 116/855663**

It was a dull September day in 1942. Hugh Edwards, the tenant of Rhos-y-Mawn farm was worried – the last of the harvest had yet to be brought in and the elevator on the binder had broken. By mid-day though, all was fixed and the green Fordson tractor had trundled off with the binder, leaving Hugh to pile the sheaves of corn into stooks. This backbreaking task was interrupted by the untimely arrival of an ailing Wellington bomber which, lacking the vital power needed to sustain flight, crash-landed about 200 yards away.

With the hot engines creaking as they cooled, the crew stepped calmly from the wreckage where Hugh joined them as they lit up cigarettes, chatting amiably. The pilot told Hugh that they had lost power whilst on a navigational exercise to Great Orme's Head and casually mentioned that this was, indeed, the second crash landing he had successfully accomplished.

**This Wellington suffered a similiar fate to BJ700. The dingy has popped from its housing in the starboard wing and inflated.**

A passing, but heavy, shower put a damper on this little tête à tête so the crew nonchalantly retired to the relative comfort of the virtually undamaged fuselage. Emerging from their shelter after the rain, someone suggested that, as the ground was saturated with 100 octane petrol from the ruptured fuel tanks, it might be a good idea if they extinguished their cigarettes!

Meanwhile, PC Davies the local policeman had, from his small station house at Llangernyw, informed the authorities of the occurrence. About two hours later RAF transport arrived and the crew departed for, as far as Hugh was concerned, an unknown destination.

An RAF guard kept souvenir hunters at bay but nearly three weeks elapsed before the aircraft was completely dismantled. It was then taken away on three 'Queen Mary' articulated trailers; engines and ancillaries on one, wings on another and the fuselage on a third.

This was the second RAF crash landing in the Elwy Valley where the crew had escaped unharmed but, before the war had come to a close, two more crashes were to exact a terrible toll when all twelve crew members were killed.

The above information was obtained entirely from the description given by eye-witnesses at the time of the event and those who saw the evidence later. Without knowing the aircraft serial number I was unable to pursue the matter further. Police Constable Davies did not note the number at the time and Police Records now held in the County Archives, apart from mentioning a crash one and a half miles south west of Llangernyw, do not record the type and number of the aeroplane.

I spent several weeks attempting to discover this number to no avail, so it was with some relief that the official report of the accident was finally unearthed at the RAF museum. (On whose research facilities I rely heavily.)

An increasing number of aircrew were coming to Bomber Command from Canada and in 1942 RCAF squadrons, all numbered in the 400 series, were being formed. Initially in No 4 Group, they were, later in 1942, gathered together in the mainly Canadian No 6 Group, officially becoming operational on 1st January 1943. No 425, one of the first Canadian squadrons, was still under the aegis of No 4 Group in September 1942 and working up to operational status. This involved flying navigational and bombing exercises in the Wellington lll aircraft which were to form their initial equipment.

BJ700, one of a batch of six hundred machines built at the Broughton factory, was allocated to the newly formed 425 squadron.

At about mid-day on 23rd September 1942, R93197 Sgt G Cronk (RCAF) took-off in BJ700 from his base at Dishforth, Yorks, with a crew of five. They were on a navigational exercise and fuel consumption test over North Wales. Just before 4 pm severe icing conditions were encountered, causing one of the Hercules engines to ice up. (A condition not unknown on the Wellington.)

Sgt Cronk nursed the aircraft along on the remaining engine, which soon began to overheat and lose power, making a landing imperative. The pilot executed an extremely skilful landing in the sloping field. (At least as difficult as that made by L4230, described elsewhere in this book.)

Despite the saving of six valuable lives, those in authority at Dishforth looking into this event were not impressed. They concluded that the pilot had failed to carry out correct single engine flying procedures, which caused the engine to overheat. No word of praise for poor Sgt Cronk! It was also mentioned that the pilot retracted the undercarriage after the engine failure but they did not elaborate on the reason for it being down in the first place. (Perhaps they meant *lowered* the undercarriage.)

The incident, only dealt with at Station level and not referred to Group or Command, was put down to pilot inexperience.

As nothing further is known of Sgt Cronk and his crew, let us fervently hope that they survived the operational flying awaiting them in what was to be Bomber Command's most turbulent period.

The exact position of the crash is in no doubt as Hugh Edwards could see the wreckage from the farm gate during the three weeks of its sojourn on his land. He has now retired to Rhos-on-Sea but the present incumbent gave me permission to search the field. (Small fields being unsuitable for cereal production, the land has now been returned to pasture.)

The search was likely to be unproductive in view of the completeness of the wreckage, nevertheless, I was determined to try to find something. The occupants of the field did not seem to encourage this venture; a large bull and a number of sizable bullocks stood idling their time away in a corner. The gate was, however, in a dip, out of sight of these creatures, so I strode confidently down the meadow. Moments later the earth behind

**Crash site through the farm gate.**

**A 'Queen Mary' – Bedford truck with a Tasker Trailer carries the fuselage of a Vickers Valetta, which succeeded the Wellington T10 in service.**

me shook as the bullocks, on some bovine whim, decided to rush to the other side of the field. The thunder of their hooves reminding me momentarily, of a stampede scene in some Western film. They had not seen me and were out of my sight again – but had effectively cut off my line of retreat. At this point I decided that the interests of self-preservation took precedence over site investigation so hurriedly made my way to a nearby wood, contenting myself with viewing the crash site from a safe distance.

To those who may criticise my lack of moral fibre I should add that, when speaking to the farmer afterwards, I asked him whether it was in fact safe to go into that particular field. He gave me a quizzical look and a non-committally, 'We-ll... they are bulls aren't they?' Perhaps I should have asked him first!

***Oxford Mk1 N4568, No.11 Flying Training School, on a training flight from Shawbury, crashed 3rd August 1941 at Sychnant Pass.***

**Crash site map numbe**

**Map reference 115/755769**

In the years preceding the Second World War there were many small aircraft companies in Britain. Most of these traded almost from day to day, relying on orders mostly in single figures. Airspeed of Portsmouth was established in 1931 by four partners, one of whom was Neville Shute Norway, later to become the famous author writing novels in which aircraft and the industry figured prominently. This company was one of those which not only survived this difficult period but manufactured aircraft of their own design throughout the war. They were also responsible for designing the RAF's first operational troop-carrying glider, the Horsa.

After the war Airspeed brought out the handsome twin-engined Ambassador airliner which stunned spectators, myself included, with a display at the Farnborough air show. This, including take-off, was entirely carried out on one engine. The Ambassador, although used by BEA, was overtaken by the jet and turbo prop era. Development costs could no longer be sustained by small companies and the Airspeed name, together with many others, disappeared from the scene.

In 1934 Airspeed designed and built the Envoy, a small twin-engined passenger aircraft which soon earned itself a reputation for reliability. The RAF ordered seven, one of which, L7270, was allocated to the King's Flight. When specification T23/36 was issued by the Air Ministry for a twin-engined trainer, a militarised version of the Envoy, renamed Oxford, filled the bill and an order for 136 was placed.

This was the start of a production run, sub-contracted to Percival, de Havilland and Standard Motors, which, when manufacture ended in July 1945, had supplied 8586 aircraft for use in Canada, New Zealand, Rhodesia and South Africa in addition to home units. USAAF units in Britain also took delivery of one hundred and thirty two aircraft for communications duties.

At the outbreak of war the Oxford was used to deal with most aspects of aircrew training. This included gunnery, for which a dorsal turret was provided. On later aircraft however, the turret was deleted, the aircraft being used for pilot training and communications.

The Oxford 1 was powered by two Armstrong-Siddeley Cheetah X 375 hp radial engines, giving it a maximum speed of 188 mph and a seven hundred mile range.

N 4568, one of a batch of 200 aircraft built by the de Havilland company, was based at No 11 FTS Shawbury.

**USAAF personnel refuel an Oxford from an RAF bowser. They used over 130 of the type in a pilot training and communication role.**

**An unknown Sergeant Pilot at the controls of an Oxford.**

The first few solo flights by any pilot must be rather tense. Without the reassuring presence of the instructor, ready to take control should things get out of hand, nerves must, surely, be tested to the limit.

Of course the pilot of N 4568 had already gone solo on single-engined aircraft and it appears, by studying his records, that this may not have been his first multi-engined flight alone. It is certainly revealed that 1076375 Leading Aircraftsman T W Gurnell had only flown three hours solo in Oxfords up to the time of his death. Whether these were all on his final flight is not clear, but that he was not yet qualified is evident by his rank of LAC. (Sergeant was the lowest rank of qualified pilot.) He had flown a total of sixty five hours whilst under training and only twenty nine of these were solo.

On the morning of 3rd August 1941, LAC Gurnell started his take-off run in Oxford

N 4568, during which the aircraft swung violently to starboard, passing the watch office (control tower) at about twenty feet. The Court of Inquiry later concluded that this caused the pilot 'some agitation' which made him leave the local area.

This was intended to be a practice flight in the circuit area, presumably involving 'Circuits and Bumps' or rollers. (Landing without stopping and then taking-off again immediately.)

Climbing above the cloud, it appears that he became totally lost, straying some sixty miles to the north west from his base. The weather had deteriorated, with a cloud base less than 1,000 feet and the Oxford pilot must now, I imagine, have become thoroughly demoralised. He had not, apparently, tried to obtain assistance by radio, before plunging into the mountainside at the head of the Sychnant Pass, near Conwy. (My friend, former Mustang pilot, Wing Commander 'Sam' Wheller (RAF Rtd) suggested that, even had the radio been working, it may well have been impossible to obtain a 'fix' in that area in 1941.)

The aircraft, mainly of wooden construction, caught fire and burnt out, killing the pilot instantly.

Who can tell what feelings of terror and solitude LAC Gurnell must have suffered as the roar of the engines took him inexorably to his lonely death.

He died for freedom as surely as any pilot on an operational squadron.

* * * * * *

The hillside is easily found and frequently used by walkers and horse riders. Almost opposite is the Sychnant Pass Hotel, where the present owner (who, by one of those amazing coincidences,

**The crash site in the foreground with the sea and Llandudno in the distance. The building is the Sychnant Pass Hotel.**

flew on the same aircraft and squadron as the author) directed me to some local people to gain further information. This, however, proved a futile exercise, as memories were blurred by the parachute descent in 1944, and in the same area, by the crew of Halifax HR723 which crashed at Pydew.

I then contacted David Haynes, a local historian, for help. Mr Haynes got in touch with someone living in Dwgyfylchi who, as a boy, remembers lads from the village climbing the mountain track and returning with various fragments from the aircraft. Using his description of the area, a map reference was calculated and I began a search which was to take many months.

The first three visits produced a number of fired 0.303 inch and 0.300 calibre rounds with crimped ends typical of blank ammunition. These were not really evidence of an air crash but more likely to be wartime army training exercises.

Finally, on my last visit, after a total of nine hours searching, I found a bare patch in the bracken. Here a number of small aircraft remains were unearthed including, incredibly, fragments of paint showing that some of the normal yellow 'trainer' finish had been overpainted with dark green.

**Only minute fragments now remain.**

***Anson 1 N5130, No.8(0) AFU, on a navigational exercise from Mona, crashed 15th February 1944 at Marl Farm.***

**Crash site map number 8 Map reference 115/797791**

Many hundreds of Ansons were lost during the war but few because of reliability problems; it was a sturdy craft. Not a great number to enemy action either for it was in the training role that the Anson, as related elsewhere in this volume, made its mark.

Most accidents were the result of errors in navigation, compounded by the unforgiving geography of Wales over which many training flights took place. Two navigation schools, Nos 8 and 9 (0) AFUs were based at three airfields in North West Wales. Here, at Penrhos, Llandwrog and Mona, a combined total of some one hundred and twenty Anson aircraft were on strength.

It would be wrong to blame the navigators for the errors which resulted in these accidents; they were still learning their skills, and mistakes using equipment which by today's standards was primitive, were inevitable.

Having made the above observations, it is interesting to note that none of the three particular Anson crashes described in this book were, in fact, due to faulty navigation!

One of a batch of five hundred aircraft built by A V Roe, N5130 was delivered to No 9 Maintenance Unit RAF on 25th April 1939. After serving at six training units, twice sustaining damage in flying accidents, it finally arrived at RAF Mona, Anglesey, on 11th December 1943. Eleven weeks later it crashed, with the loss of all five crew members.

On 15th February 1944, Anson N5130 took-off from RAF Mona on a cross-country navigational exercise. At the controls was F Sgt M Samuels, a pilot with over three hundred hours solo to his credit, one hundred and twenty eight of these on Ansons.

At 1535 hours, whilst flying near Llandudno, part of a wing broke off and the aircraft plummeted to the ground at Marl Farm on the outskirts of the town.

As was usual in such cases, the wreckage was carefully sifted through in order to establish the cause but no positive conclusion could be reached. That the wing failed there was no doubt but the reason for it having done so was unclear. The AIB noted that the cause was unknown, suggesting that it could have resulted from an elevator breaking away from the wing. Incidents of a similar nature had been reported prior to this tragedy, but the accident rate had remained extremely low. The C O nevertheless recommended that, in future, periodic overhauls of the structures involved should be made by contractors.

* * * * *

Since the crash, some fifty four years ago, a main road has been driven through the site, providing more direct access to Llandudno. I made a close search of the area, together with adjacent woodland but nothing came to light. In 1997 council engineering work was carried out on the site, so I was able to speak to JCB operators but they could not recall finding anything unusual. This work and the proliferation of rubbish in the nearby wood makes it extremely unlikely that anything will ever be recovered.

**Crash site of Anson N5130. Because of recent engineering work it is unlikely that any remains will come to light.**

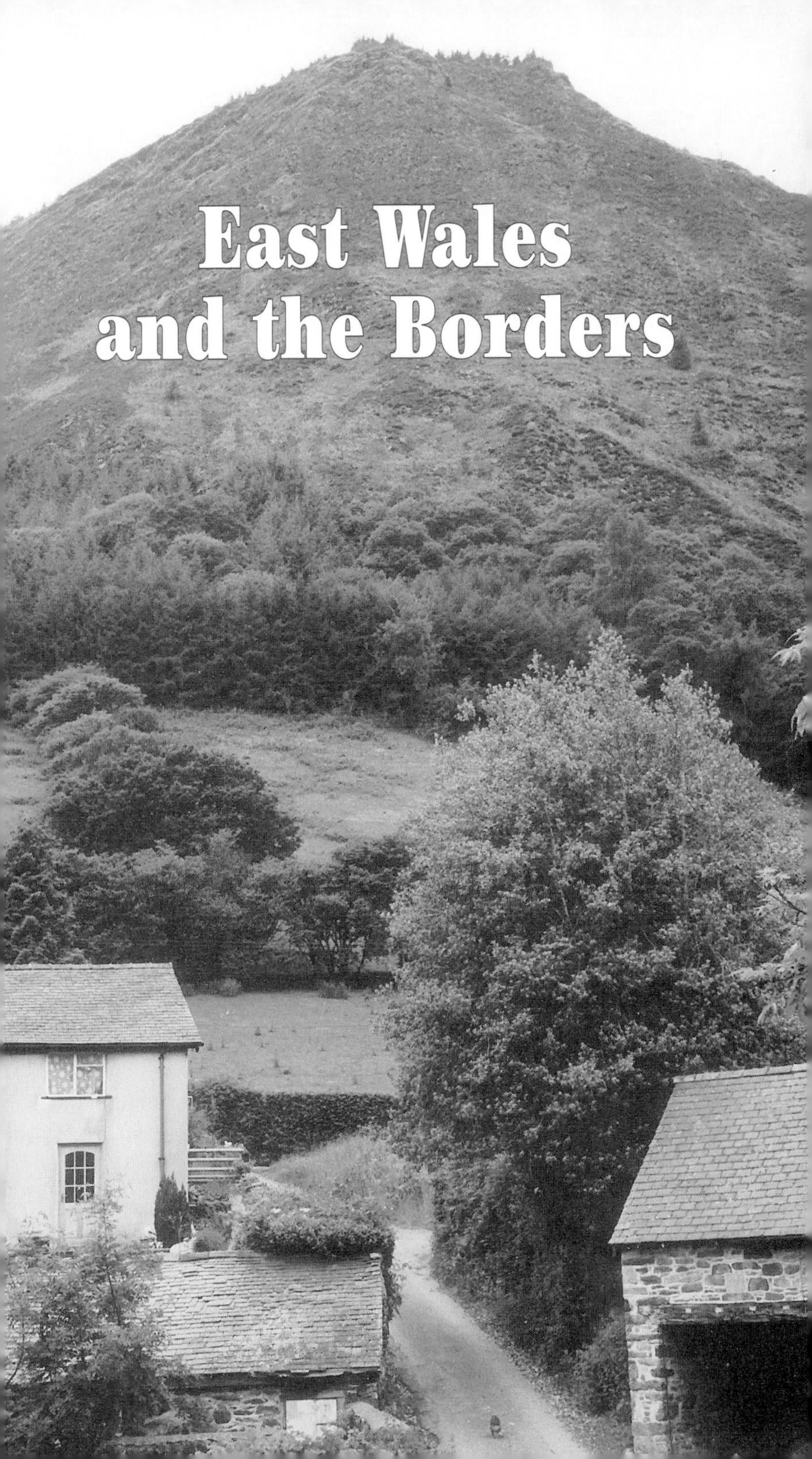

# East Wales and the Borders

# THE WORLD'S END

To the north of the Vale of Llangollen lies a mountainous region which extends for over five miles. It is reached by taking the scenic road to the Horseshoe Pass from Llangollen and then branching off onto a minor road, following signposts to World's End. Although Wrexham is only half a dozen miles away to the north east, it really does seem like the end of the world, a rocky escarpment to the right giving the impression of entering a remote mountainous area.

In fact, the highest point in the entire range is only about 1900 feet. The southern part is known as Ruabon mountain, whilst that to the north Esclusham or Minera mountain. These are not really mountains at all but high moorlands deep in heather. The Minera end of the range was extensively mined in the past and walkers must beware of remaining shafts. To the north, low ground extends to the Dee estuary, whilst to the east it drops down to Wrexham and the flat fields of Cheshire beyond.

Though not great in height, the region is often shrouded in mist or low cloud and, because of this, many aircraft met their end in these hills.

From a point at approximately MR117/232484, a path can be seen climbing quite steeply to the right of the road. This is a good starting point for a visit to two crash sites, which can be found in a couple of hours. (If you are lucky, that is!) Both, surrounded by deep heather, can only be seen when almost on top of them and I would suggest visiting these sites from north to south. Only that to the north comes anywhere near mine workings, which are clearly signed and recognised by spoil heaps nearby.

Although, initially, you take the path as stated, you must leave it after fifteen minutes or so and stride off in a northerly direction through the heather. (Perhaps 'stumble' would be a better word!)

This area presents an interesting challenge to the searcher. It is unlikely that you will discover both sites on your first visit, so to find just one must be counted a success.

***Spitfire XVIe TE210, 631 Squadron, on a routine training flight from Llanbedr, crashed 31st August 1945 on Minera Mountain.***

**Crash site map number 9 Map reference 117/242489**

The Spitfire is probably the most famous aircraft ever built. It served in the RAF at a most crucial period of its history, from 1938 to 1951, a total of 20,351 aircraft being produced. Two types of engine, the Rolls-Royce Merlin and, in later marks, the Griffon were used by the Spitfire during this time. Power rose from 1030 hp, in 1938, to 2050 when the war ended, while maximum speed increased from 355 to 460 mph.

The Mark XVl was, in reality, a Mark lX but with an American Packard-built Merlin 266 engine of 1720 hp. A large number of Spitfires had clipped wings for better manoeuvrability at low level; often known as 'clipped, cropped and clapped'. 'Cropped' referred to the shortened supercharger blades and 'clapped' to the fact that performance was reduced at higher levels. The Mark XVle utilised the 'e' type wing in which the 0.303 inch machine guns were replaced by those of 0.5 inch calibre.

631 squadron was formed on 1st December 1943, at Tywyn, by the amalgamation of numbers 1605 and 1628 Flights of No 1 Anti-aircraft Co-operation Unit. Earlier in the war this unit operated the Hawker Henley, towing targets for the A A gunners at nearby Tonfanau but, by 1945, the underpowered Henley had been replaced by the Vultee Vengeance, a powerful American dive bomber. The Spitfires were used for gunnery calibration. After the end of hostilities, the squadron moved to Llanbedr, an airfield with more permanent facilities.

Spitfire XVle TE210 left the Castle Bromwich works on 10th May 1945; just over three months later it was destroyed, sadly killing the pilot in the process.

On 31st August 1945 Pilot Officer Frank Fendley took off in TE210 on a routine training flight and, for reasons which will probably never be known, struck the northern part of Minera Mountain. Often, in cases like this, the cause can be attributed to radio failure, which prevents the pilot from getting a fix for return to base. He is then faced with the dilemma of when to descend through cloud to find his position, whilst only too well aware that a slight error of navigation, at 300 mph, can prove fatal.

A few panels and various fragments lie in a hollow in the heather covered hillside at this site. Some of the larger pieces can be identified by the '300' serial number prefix. A compass bearing can then be taken to the next MR, where the Beaufighter wreckage can be found.

**Wreckage of TE210 on the bracken covered moorland.**

**A quick clean reveals serial numbers on this piece of engine cowling panel.**

| Type of Aircraft | Mark | R.A.F. Number |
| --- | --- | --- |
| | LF XVI | TE 210 |

| Contractor | Contract No. | Engine installed :— |
| --- | --- | --- |
| V-A CB | B 981687/39 | MERLIN 266 |
| | | Maker's airframe No. :— |

| Unit or Cat'y/Cause | Station or Contractor | Date | Authority | 41 ~~or 43~~ Gp. Allot. |
| --- | --- | --- | --- | --- |
| 27.4.45 | 19 MU | 30.4.45 | 75 | 55050 |
| | Vickers CB | 10.5.45 | 31 | |
| | 9 MU | 30.5.45 | 14 | |
| | 631 Sqd | 11.8.45 | 83 | |
| 31.8.45 | FA Cat E | | Sig 42/31 | |
| | SOC | [illegible] | [illegible] | |

A.M. Form 78

**The Movement card made out for Spitfire TE210 indicating a catagory E – totally destroyed.**

***Beaufighter TFX NE203, Air Transport Auxiliary, on a delivery flight from Weston to Inverness, crashed 3rd November 1943 on Minera Mountain.***

**Crash site map number 10 Map reference 117/243483**

During the war, thousands of new and repaired aircraft had to be collected from various factories and delivered to RAF squadrons. It would have placed an unacceptable burden on those squadrons, in wartime, if their own pilots had been taken off operations to carry out this task. In the event, the Air Transport Auxiliary, a civilian organisation, had this respons-ibility.

The ATA, although planned in 1938, actually came into existence the day war broke out. Its members were required to have a minimum of five hundred flying hours' experience but it was not always an enviable task. Many different types of aircraft had to be flown, some by pilots with only a minimum training on a specific type.

The Operational Record Books together with Accident Investigation Branch reports of events taking place over thirty years ago, are available for public scrutiny at the PRO Kew. These, in the case of accident reports, give details of the incidents in great detail; too much detail, perhaps, for general readership. Were they to be quoted in full, this book would have to be of much greater extent.

It would be of interest, nevertheless, to include one chapter where the report is studied at length, if only to show that, even at the height of the war, crashes were not just taken for granted.

THE PILOT

No 828169 Flight Sergeant J Shepherd was an RAF pilot seconded to the ATA for ferry duties. The Chief Instructor of the ATA had made the following comments on his history card.

> *'This pilot came to us from the RAF with a little over two hundred hours on light types: Oxfords, Blenheims and Beaufighters. His Class 1 training was rather slow and, although he showed average ability, his judgement and airmanship were not very consistent.*

**A Beaufighter TFX with torpedo.**

*He was posted to the Air Ferry Training School for a conversion course where he did quite well but was inclined to hurry his cockpit checks and other routines. In training pool he did his work steadily and quietly and, although not one to push himself to the front, he proved himself a useful and quiet member of the team.*

*This pilot must remember the weaknesses in the early period of his training as such failings can quickly lead to accidents if they are allowed to persist during ferrying'.*

THE AIRCRAFT

'Beaufighter NE203 was assembled by BAC Weston-Super-Mare and had flown for forty five minutes prior to take-off on 3rd November 1943. This period of forty five minutes consisted of three flights by the firm's test pilot, but only minor between flight adjustments were carried out.

NE203 was fitted with full rocket gear, torpedo release and one rearward machine gun. Both engines were installed during manufacture and had not been used previously'.

THE FLIGHT AND AFTERMATH

This aircraft, with Flight Sergeant Shepherd at the controls, took off from Weston airfield at approximately 1400 hours on 3rd November 1943 on a delivery flight to Inverness, via Kirkbride. It is believed that the pilot intended to proceed by the Severn Valley but nothing further is known of the aircraft's movements until it crashed on high ground in Wales.

The aircraft struck the ground when diving in a slightly over the vertical attitude and did not fly into the hillside. Both engines were buried to a depth of about six feet and the airframe was completely destroyed by impact and subsequent fire. The mark of the leading edge of the wings could be clearly traced, both wing tips being found in their respective positions. The fuselage was completely destroyed, with the exception of the rear end and tail assembly. This unit was found about 30 feet from the point of first impact. No eye-witness statements are available but two lumbermen, who were working nearby, heard an aircraft swishing through the air, apparently with the engines off. After this noise continued for two or three seconds there was a bang and, on running in the direction of the sound, they found the

**A South African Air Force Beaufighter attacking a German target in Yugoslavia in this, possibly among the best wartime images of a 'Beau' in action.**

**NE203 was fitted with full rocket gear, torpedo release and one rearward machine gun.**

wreckage of a burning aircraft. Visibility at the time was bad and, at the site of the accident, was restricted to approximately 150 yards.

RESULT OF THE INVESTIGATION

*'The pilot had signed as having read the route forecast which was given as: Mainly cloudy, occasional rain or showers, 8 to 10 tenths cloud at 1-2000 feet but generally 10 tenths at 600 to 1000 feet. Freezing level 7000 feet, icing index high.*

*On inspection of the crash site it was possible to establish that no major structural failure had occurred prior to impact. All large detachable panels were identified and found in good order, apart from fire and impact damage. Damage to engines and props was consistent with impact and none of these units showed any signs of fire in the air.*

*Both artificial horizon and turn and bank gyros were recovered but neither showed any obvious signs of spinning at time of impact. In view of the very extensive fire damage, however, too much reliance should not be placed on this evidence. It is noted that the pivots on the artificial horizon rotor were slightly grooved and this matter is being investigated.*

*This accident was caused by loss of control but the reason for this has not been established. ATA Standing Orders are that pilots should, at all times, maintain visual contact with the ground and it is clear that F Sgt Shepherd was not complying with this instruction. ATA personnel are not given instruction in instrument flying but it is possible that Shepherd, who was trained by the RAF, may have got into difficulties whilst attempting to go over the top.'*

The above is a shortened version of a precis of the accident report, so it can be seen that the matter was gone into most thoroughly.

Today, only a few pathetic remains, some stamped with Bristol prefixes, are all that can be found of NE203 on the windswept moorland. One is reminded that pilots such as Flight Sergeant Shepherd died just as surely while performing these routine, but essential, tasks as on active service against the enemy.

**The few remaining remnants of NE203 lying amidst the heather.**

***Blenheim MkIV L4873, 17 Operational Training Unit, on a formation flying exercise from Upwood, crashed 23rd March 1940 on Foel Wen.***

**Crash site map number 11 Map reference 125/102324**

In 1933, Bristol's chief designer, Frank Barnwell, designed a twin-engined, high speed monoplane with seats for six passengers. Lord Rothermere, the *Daily Mail* proprietor was so taken with the aeroplane that he ordered one, but with more powerful Bristol Mercury engines of 840 hp.

The *Daily Mail* had long been a keen proponent of air travel, indeed, it was in it's issue of 5th October 1908 that a prize of

**The Bristol 'Britain First' from which the Blenheim evolved.**

**The prototype Bristol Blenheim, a development from the Britain First.**

£1000 was offered for the first crossing of the English Channel by aeroplane. This, as is well known, was won by Louis Bleriot on 25th July 1909.

This new aircraft, the Type 142, was named 'Britain First' and first flew on 12th April 1935. It was then sent to the Aircraft and Armament Experimental Establishment at Martlesham Heath, Suffolk, for acceptance trials.

'Britain First' caused somewhat of a sensation, for it was much faster than the RAF's fighters of the day and remained so for some time. The Air Council thought that it would make a good light bomber so Lord Rothermere presented it to the RAF where it was given the serial number K7557. From this was developed the Blenheim, which first flew just over a year later.

By the outbreak of war, the Mark 1 version had been mostly superseded in the UK by the Mark IV. This aircraft. powered by Bristol Mercury XV engines of 920 hp, had a maximum speed of 266 mph and could carry 1320 lbs of bombs.

On July 4th 1941, Wing Commander H. Edwards, an Australian of Welsh ancestry, won the VC during a daylight raid on Bremen in a Blenheim. Four of the twelve Blenheims of 105 squadron were lost on this operation. During a six month period of the same year Blenheims sank more than 70 ships.

The last Blenheim operation with Bomber Command was on 18th August 1942, although it continued to serve overseas for some time after. They were not consigned to the scrap-heap however, but to the Middle East and OTU's where they were already being used extensively.

Blenheim L4873 was operated by 90 squadron and was one of the first to be delivered in March 1939. It was then passed on to 17 OTU. based at Upwood near Huntingdon. That is, if we are to

**The crash site of L4873 with Mynydd Tarw in background.**

believe the official crash record. Some publications state that it was still on the strength of 90 squadron, whilst others put it's point of departure as RAF Shawbury. It is much more likely, however, that those who made the Accident Report knew where they were located at the time!

On 23rd March 1940, 562667 Sergeant M. C. Cotterell, with two other crew members, took-off in Blenheim L4873. They were accompanied by two other aircraft for a formation flying exercise to the Isle of Man and return. Over Mid-Wales the formation ran into cloud. The leader continued, but did not give correct orders to the other aircraft in accordance with the Operating Procedure; This was for the formation to separate and then climb, asking for bearings over the RT, Sergeant Cotterell put his aircraft into a gentle dive, to break cloud but struck the south-eastern slopes of Foel Wen, killing all those on board.

The later inquiry blamed the pilot for not complying with orders for formations in cloud. The formation leader, although he climbed to safety, accompanied by the other aircraft, was deemed to be too inexperienced in not ensuring that the other pilots were fully conversant with the correct procedure.

The crash site in the Berwyn mountains is one of the most beautiful and remote areas of Wales, not far from the delightful village of Llanrhaedr-Ym-Mochnant. A minor road takes you to within about a quarter of a mile of the site. An extremely steep and slippery, bracken covered slope must be tackled. It is difficult to keep upright here but well worth the effort.

Considering the 58 intervening years the amount of wreckage which remains is amazing. The hillside is littered with sizable pieces which can easily be photographed and even in some cases, identified.

**Wing main spar.**

**Front hatch release handle.**

***B17E 41-9098, 97th Bomb Group, from Polebrook to Burtonwood, crashed 11th August 1942 on Craig Berwyn.***

**Crash site map number 12 Map reference 125/078334**

Of the twelve thousand seven hundred and sixty one Flying Fortresses built, only five hundred and twelve were of the 'E' variant. Prior to this one hundred and nineteen aircraft of B, C and D models were produced.

The first twenty B17Cs were ordered by the British Purchasing Commission in Washington, ostensibly for use by the

**B17C in RAF service with 90 Squadron in 1941.**

RAF as training aircraft. The US knew full well that they would be used operationally but hoped to benefit by the experience thus gained.

These aircraft were, however, flown in a way not envisaged by the Americans, that is in small groups at very high altitude. The first RAF operation was on 8th July 1941. The first loss, when an aircraft crashed on return to base, was on 11th August and the first aircraft shot down, on 8th September 1941. On the 25th September one aircraft was despatched to Emden, but was forced to turn back.

This was the last Bomber Command operation by B17Cs. They had achieved little success in the hands of 90 squadron and had proved vulnerable to attack, especially from the rear. The bomb load was small and the aircraft cost was high in terms of cash, crews and maintenance.

These lessons were quickly learned by Boeing so, consequently, the B17E was virtually a new aircraft. Extra guns, power operated turrets and aerodynamic changes transformed the Fortress. Nevertheless, only five hundred and twelve 'E' models were built and it was the last B17 built solely by Boeing; from then on Douglas and Lockhead-Vega joined in producing, between them, almost as many aircraft as Boeing itself.

The first formation of USAAF B17Es began their journey to Europe on 18th June 1942, when they flew to Presque Island on the north east tip of Maine. They resumed their journey at 1625 on the 26th, when fifteen of these aircraft took off for Bluie West in Greenland, via Goose Bay, Labrador. The weather clamped in and eleven returned to Goose after fourteen hours airborne, one arrived at Bluie, while the remaining three crash landed but with no casualties.

After a 2965 mile flight, 41-9085 was the first aircraft to arrive in the UK, at Prestwick. The remaining aircraft followed soon afterwards but not without loss; five B17s together with six P38s accompanying them, came to grief although all crews survived.

On 6th July 1942, four aircraft from Prestwick landed at Polebrook and continued on to Grafton Underwood near Kettering, to form the nucleus of the 97th Bomb Group. The first operation took place only forty two days later and in this period the 340th Bomb Squadron embarked on a programme of intensive training, as some of the crew members had not

**B-17Gs in action over Germany.**

completed their training in the US.

Weather conditions here were rather different from those to which they had become accustomed in the USA and the first B17 loss in the UK occurred during this period.

41-9098 was accepted by the USAAF on 8th April 1942. Both aircraft and engines had been operated for a total of only 230 hours at the time of the accident.

On 11th August the crew of 41-9098 was detailed for a flight to Burtonwood near Warrington. The pilot was Second Lieutenant Henry L. Gilbert who, in the two months prior to August, had flown nearly one hundred hours on B17s (a not inconsiderable amount). His crew consisted of:

| | |
|---|---|
| 2/Lt R. Beers | Co-pilot |
| 2/Lt L Schmitt | Navigator |
| 2/Lt L. Phillips | Bombadier |
| M/Sgt S. Lepa | Gunner |
| S/Sgt R. Kemp | Radio Operator |
| Sgt K. Branom | Gunner |
| Sgt W. Sidders | Gunner |

Passengers:

| | |
|---|---|
| Cpl M Koepke | Crew Chief |
| Cpl S Aldridge | Aerial engineer |
| Pvt F Villarreal | Assistant crew chief |

The weather report advised that a cold front was moving in with heavy rain, visibility of two miles and a ceiling of 1000 feet. At 0945 S/Sgt J Phillips of Group Operations gave clearance for the flight to proceed; at 1030 hours Lieutenant Gilbert and his crew took off from Polebrook, with an ETA at Burtonwood of 1100.

At about 1100 hrs, 41-9098 crashed into Craig Berwyn at the north east extremity of the Cadair Berwyn range, which rises over 2000 feet. The aircraft burst into flames on impact and all

**A bare patch on the hillside marks the crash site of 41-9098.**

crew members and passengers were killed.

The subsequent inquiry into this, the first loss of a B-17 in the European Theatre of Operations, concluded that pilot error was responsible due to his lack of experience in bad weather flying. A more experienced pilot cleared to the same destination at about the same time, decided to turn back because of poor visibilty. The Inquiry recommended that inexperienced pilots be warned of their responsibilities as crew commanders, and that their limitations as pilots be stressed.

Today, a look at the map of the area will show that the Berwyns are well to the west of the track to Burtonwood; the aircraft should have been flying considerably higher than 2500 feet had they been taking a westerly route. The fact that they had travelled a little over half-way to their destination, descending to below 2000 feet, seems to indicate that they were hopelessly lost. There do not appear to be any records available now to explain why no radio messages were sent informing either Burtonwood or Polebrook of their plight. Indeed, the documents show that their non-arrival was only reported at 1400 hours. Why the delay? We can only surmise. Perhaps in the early days the ground organisation had not yet geared itself up for such circumstances.

During the years since the disaster many people, especially those in eastern England, where the majority of the Eighth Air Force's bases were located, have become interested in sites of USAAF 'mishaps' as they were rather quaintly known.

The amount of wreckage surviving is almost nil and finding the exact locations frequently becomes a problem. I had passed by this particular site before, whilst on a fruitless search for wreckage of other aircraft, but without even noticing it. It was not until a friend obtained further information that I was successful, map reading having been made rather a problem because a forest, shown on the Ordnance Survey map, had been recently felled.

All that can now be seen is a large, bare, brown patch on the hillside. This lies about 350 yards to the left of the footpath which rises quite steeply towards Cadair Bronwen. Nevertheless, the ground is littered with small fragments of airframe and other pieces. With no serial numbers to be seen identification is, of course, difficult, especially as a number of other aircraft crashed nearby in the Berwyns.

Eventually, a round of 0.300 inch ammunition was found, together with a fragment of rubber piping about four inches long. This still bore the red seal of the US Rubber Company, with serial number stamped into it.

The 0.300 exploded round was a most lucky find; British aircraft did not use this calibre and, indeed, the B17E only carried one gun of this size, mounted in the nose.

**Small fragments of 41-9098 including rubber hose with manufacturers stamp.**

***Washington B1 WF502, 90 Squadron, Marham, on exercise Kingpin, crashed 8th January 1953 near Llanarmon-Yn-Ial.***

**Crash site map number 13 Map reference 116/179542**

In Europe, by 1944, the B17s and B24s of the USAAF combined with RAF Bomber Command to lay waste the industrial cities of the Third Reich. The war against Japan, however, was a different matter entirely. Ranges involved here were far greater and no Allied bomber had the capability to bridge them. On the stocks in Boeing's plant in Seattle the B17s successor, the B29, was being prepared.

A great advance on the Flying Fortress (B17) the B29 had a wing span of 141 feet, all up weight of 135,000 lbs and a bomb load of up to 12,000 lbs. More important than all of this was its range of 3,250 miles. Powered by four Wright Cyclone 18 cylinder radial engines, of 2200 hp each, it could attain a maximum speed of 375 mph. With its defensive armament of ten 0.5 inch machine guns, it was a formidable fighting machine.

Even so, it was not until the Mariana Islands, some 1,500 miles from the Japanese mainland, were captured that the bombing campaign against Japan could begin. This culminated in the dropping of the atomic bomb on Hiroshima, so it would probably be true to say that the B29 was responsible for saving countless thousands of US servicemen's lives and considerably shortening the war.

The B29 first flew on 21st September 1942, and when production ended, in August 1945, one thousand and fifty six had been produced. In 1950 the RAF was equipped with ageing Lincoln bombers, delivery of the new jet-propelled 'V' bombers being still some way off. Because of the pressures of the Cold War, it was decided that eighty eight USAF B29s should be taken out of storage, as an interim measure, for use by the RAF. In Bomber Command the B29 was to be known as the Washington. (In the US Air Forces, aircraft were and still are, usually known by their designations, thus the B17, B24 and F111 etc. In the RAF, aircraft are invariably given names, and American aircraft purchased for British use were no exception. The names given often reflected their place of origin, for instance, Maryland, Baltimore, Catalina and Washington.)

Eight squadrons were so equipped, the first delivery being in March 1952 but by 1954, with the large scale introduction into

**Air and ground crews with their Washington.**

service of the Canberra, they had been returned to the USA. (The Canberra was a modern day equivalent of the Mosquito and had to fill the role of a strategic bomber, a task for which it was not designed.)

In 1953, No 90 squadron, 3 Group, Bomber Command, was based at Marham, Norfolk and involved in many exercises consisting of simulated radar and visual bombing attacks, often exceeding sixteen hours in duration. One such exercise was codenamed 'Kingpin', to be carried out on the night of 8th January 1953.

The crew of Washington WF 502 was one of those detailed for this exercise. As the regular pilot was indisposed, his place was taken by the Flight Commander S Ldr W J Sloane. He was an above average pilot, with 3,000 flying hours to his credit, including over 500 on the Washington.

His crew was:

| | | |
|---|---|---|
| P O | C B SPELLER | Co-pilot |
| P O | S LIGHTOWLER | Navigator |
| Sgt | E D PEARTON | Navigator 2 |
| Sgt | A MARTIN | Engineer |
| Sgt | R ANDERSON | Signaller |
| F Sgt | K A REAKES | Gunner |
| Sgt | R G HUGHSON | Gunner |
| Sgt | E F WHEELER | Gunner |
| Sgt | M J CLINTON | Gunner |

WF 502 lifted off from Marham at 1440 hours, carrying out its planned attacks from 19,000 feet. After approximately six and a half hours flying, the aircraft suddenly plunged down, breaking up before hitting the ground near Llanarmon-Yn-Ial and scattering wreckage in a long narrow path for about five miles. All ten crew members were killed outright.

The initial Inquiry found that the aircraft had broken up whilst in a steep dive and that the major section of wreckage struck the ground in a stalled, inverted condition. The reason why the aircraft was flying at low level when it should have been at 19,000 feet, could not be established.

The high speed dive was considered to be the primary factor in causing the crash. Structural failure, as recorded in the crash report, was consistent with airframe overstressing, due to abnormal applied airloads through the elevators in attempting a

**Press photograph taken the day after the crash showing wreckage in Wern Goed.**

high speed recovery manoeuvre.

Various components were stripped for examination but, as nothing was revealed that could account for the crash, the accident was classified as 'Miscellaneous'.

Later information which came to light seemed to indicate that the elevator control of the auto-pilot had malfunctioned, causing the aircraft to go into a steep dive, attempted recovery from which caused structural failure.

For an account of what happened on the ground at the time and after the crash I am indebted to Dr Duncan Egdell of the Llanarmon and District Conservation Society.

People heard the sound of the engines and the aircraft appeared to be circling before the crash but there was nothing to be seen in the night sky to indicate an engine or other fire. After the impact the glow in the sky appeared from the direction of Gelli Gynan and the main part of the wreckage was found in the corner of Wern Goed. Mrs Jones, of Gelli Gynan farm, was probably the first to know where the aircraft had crashed, seeing the flames from her window. Her husband and a farm worker set off across the field to the site but, as they got closer, Mr Jones saw that it was an incident of major proportions and sent the workman back to phone the emergency services.

Members of the local community reached the scene with remarkable speed. Mr Graham Hickie, who worked for de Havilland Aircraft at Broughton, set off on his motor cycle with Fred Jones on the pillion, whilst Ken Lewis arrived, clutching the fire extinguisher from his car, to find himself confronted by twenty foot tongues of flame leaping from around the wreckage. The fire, at that stage, sprang not so much from the aircraft itself but from the ground where spilt aviation fuel was burning. Some of the surrounding trees were alight and, amidst it all, was the wreckage of the forward part of the aircraft.

By the light of the flames they could see that the fuselage was relatively intact. For all they knew, people might be alive inside. Heedless of the danger, Messrs Pugh, Williams and Evans went into the fuselage, with signal cartridges exploding around them and carried out two members of the crew who were, unfortunately, dead. With a louder explosion, the rescuers retreated until joined by the emergency services.

Having arrived at Gelli Gynan farm, the firemen had to manhandle their equipment nearly a quarter of a mile across a waterlogged field. To extinguish the blazing trees, dams had to be built across streamlets to provide sufficient water.

By this time sightseers were flocking to the scene, some abandoning their cars on a narrow road so that, when other fire appliances arrived, seven cars had to be lifted bodily out of the way.

Meanwhile, PC Parry was examining the pockets of the two dead crew members, finding evidence of where they were based. Within minutes the telephone was ringing at RAF Marham, bringing them the first unwelcomed news of the fate of their Washington bomber. RAF salvage teams arrived from Valley and Hawarden, making their base at Gelli Gynan farmhouse. Here Mrs Jones kept open house throughout the night to feed and refresh the firemen, police, ambulance crews and volunteers.

The bulk of the firefighting was done by men from Ruthin and Wrexham, the former part-time firemen. Work with grappling irons continued after midnight and, by 1 am, the eighth burnt

The crash site with Gelli Gynan farmhouse in the distance.

body had been extracted.

Daylight on Friday showed that the tail, including the gun turret and other smaller wreckage, was strewn in a narrow path through Llandegla towards Llanarmon. It was not until Sunday that PC Rowlands found the remains of the tenth and last body, deep in the ashes and wreckage at Wern Goed.

Many tributes were paid at the subsequent inquests, during church services, in council chambers and elsewhere to the efforts of the emergency services and, not least, to the courageous volunteers.

The splendid hospitality provided by Mr and Mrs Jones, of Gelli Gynan farm, was recognised by senior RAF officers from Hawarden and Marham. Though simply phrased, these display a rather charming old world courtesy. One of the officers refers quaintly to '... the recent regrettable flying accident'.

The impact of such a disaster on the families of the ten crew members cannot be adequately described here. Suffice to say that Sqn Ldr Sloane left a wife and two very small children and

**A piece of tyre remains at the site.**

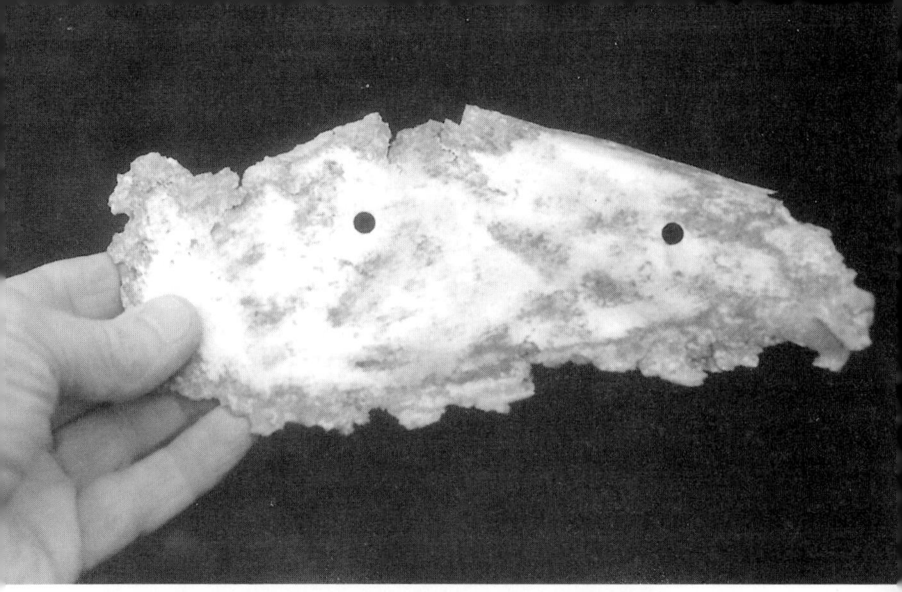

**One of the small fragments to be found scattered about.**

a tragic visitor, Mrs Margaret Reakes, came to Wern Goed two months later. This young lady was the wife of one of the air gunners and they had been married less than four months when her 28 year old husband was killed.

The main part of the wreckage fell, as stated, in Wern Goed, now belonging to nearby Pen-y-Ffrith. I was met by the present owner, David Minshull, who made me welcome and explained where I could find the exact position of the site, for my records. This was not quite so easy as expected, as this part of the wood has been felled and is covered with 'brash' (small branches and bracken) making it difficult to walk at times, let alone search. After searching for half an hour or so, much molten alloy and countless aluminium fragments came to light. Finally, part of a tyre, still showing signs of intense heat was uncovered. All was returned to its resting place. This confirmed the location of the disaster caused, most probably, by a small electrical fault but which tragically claimed the lives of ten men - casualties of the Cold War.

Never again in Wales would so many bomber crewmen be killed in a single crash; the new 'V' bombers carried no defensive armament and a crew of only five.

***Vampire T55 334, of the Iraqi Air Force on a routine delivery flight from Broughton to Hatfield, crashed 16th December 1953 at Nerquis.***

**Crash site map number 14 Map reference 117/228596**

The Vampire two-seat trainer was a simple development of the night-fighter version, with radar removed and re-location of some components. Its side-by-side seating for pupil and instructor was, at the time, considered a better system than the more usual layout where the instructor sat behind, or in front of the pupil. Having them sitting together would, it was thought, lead to their better communication. The Jet Provost and Hunter had a similar configuration. It is interesting to note that, in recent years, the RAF has returned to the original system of tandem seating, as in the Hawk and Tucano.

The engine and performance of the T55 (an export version of the RAF T11) were similar to those of the Vampire fighter. The T55 was exported to many countries from as far afield as Norway and Indonesia. The Iraqi Air Force took delivery of seven aircraft, numbered 333 to 335, 367, 386 and 388; ejector seats were not fitted to these aircraft.

In the 1950s a number of National Servicemen were trained as aircrew. This, in the case of pilots, took up most of their service and they spent little time on active squadrons.

Michael Hills-Johns (or Hilles-Johnes, reports vary on this point) was a national service pilot. On leaving the RAF as a Pilot

Officer, he joined number 500 (County of Kent) squadron Royal Auxiliary Air Force as a part-time pilot, flying the Gloster Meteor. His Commanding Officer there was Sqn Ldr Desmond de Villiers AFC, a pilot with the de Havilland Aircraft Company. It was probably through his good offices that Michael Hills-Johns (M H-J) was appointed as a delivery pilot for the same factory, a seemingly attractive position but one which was, ultimately, to cost him his life.

Living in Sutton-Vallence, near Maidstone and with a flat in London, M H-J ferried aircraft from the factory at Broughton to Hatfield and various other destinations.

On Wednesday 16th December 1953, M H-J checked his flight plan in the pilot's room at Broughton for the routine flight to Hatfield, the first leg of Vampire 334s long journey to Iraq.

Ron Metcalfe, the charge-hand mechanic, helped him with his parachute as he climbed into the cockpit. After running the

**Vampire T55 cockpit showing side-by-side instructor/trainee layout.**

engine for a few minutes, the pilot waved the chocks away and the aircraft taxied off.

At 2 pm M H-J, using his call sign Tibet 35, asked Flt Lt John Crosbie, the duty controller, for take-off clearance. At 2.04 pm he took-off normally, telling Control that he was climbing prior to setting course for Hatfield.

The scene of this tragically short drama now shifts to the ground where John Allen, of Treuddyn, was standing by the roadside near Gelli farm. Over the clouds of fog enveloping the countryside, he heard the jet approaching from the Glyndwr direction. When the aircraft seemed almost overhead he heard an explosion and was, he said, temporarily blinded by the flash. The plane '... made a terrible rattling noise' and another explosion followed as the aircraft hit the ground nearby. John was sure that the flash was not caused by the aircraft crashing and he was not alone in this observation; Harry Davies, of Pystyll farm, said that the aircraft was flying '... quite healthily' before he heard it explode in mid-air.

Back in the control office, at 2.08 pm, Flight Lieutenant Crosbie received a radio call from the pilot which, he said later, sounded '...rather hysterical'. The message was '... in cloud and out of control'. Realising that the pilot was, in Flt Lt Crosbie's words 'rather disturbed', the DCO told him that, if he really was

**Newspaper report which appeared after the inquiry.**

*Vampire crash at Nerquis*

**Pilot radioed, "Out of control and in cloud"**

"NO, NO, THIS IS IT" was the last message of Mr. Michael David Hills-Johnes, aged 23, of Parsonage Farm, Sutton Vallence, near Maidstone, a ferry pilot employed by the De Havilland Aircraft Company, Ltd., before the Vampire jet aeroplane he was flying to Hatfield crashed in a field at Ty'n Rhyn Farm, Nerquis, on December 16th. The aircraft exploded and burst into flames.

**Ty'n Rhyn Farm: crash site in foreground.**

out of control, he should leave the aircraft. The next and final message, coming almost immediately was 'No, no, this is it' followed by a long drawn out 'No'.

The aircraft crashed into a field at Ty'n Rhyn farm near Nerquis, where it exploded making a five foot deep crater and scattering fragments over a wide area. PC John Jones found the pilot's watch in the smoking crater; it was stopped at 2.09 pm. About 20 yards away lay part of M H-J's helmet.

At the subsequent Inquest various witnesses gave evidence, including Leonard Brookman chief aircraft inspector at de Havillands Broughton. He produced a certificate showing that the aircraft had been correctly test flown on four previous occasions. He had inspected the wreckage and had been unable to find any sign of fatigue or pre-crash failure. All the damage, he said, seemed to have been caused by impact with the ground.

The Coroner sat with a jury who returned a verdict of Accidental Death. Were it not for the witnesses on the ground, the evidence of the DCO and aircraft inspector would lead one to immediately think that the pilot had become disorientated in cloud and lost control. There seems, however, to be a number of independent witnesses to the fact that there was an explosion in the air. Of course, it could be that, taking the all-enveloping fog and the short time reported between the first explosion and impact into consideration, the sound became distorted, giving the impression that the explosion occurred in the air.

Again, it does seem rather glib that the DH inspector could find no sign of pre-crash failure. If descriptions of the site and photographs taken at the time are anything to go by, it would be almost impossible to form a conclusion. There was, of course, no 'black box' to provide data. Whether there was any government inquiry is not known. As it was a foreign military aircraft and no people on the ground were injured, it is possible that there was not.

So, was it pilot error or did the engine fail soon after take-off? We shall probably never know what really happened in those tragic moments elapsing between Mr Hills-Johns lifting the Vampire from the runway at Broughton and his death a mere five minutes later.

With no map reference to guide me and with Ty'n Rhyn farm not shown on OS maps, I wrote to Mrs Sara Furse, of Nerquis Hall, for assistance. She quickly put me in touch with Mr Harry Davies, the self-same person who heard the aircraft flying 'quite healthily' on that fateful December day.

I met Harry at Nerquis and he kindly invited me into his splendid old farmhouse, Pen-y-bryn. There he showed me a photograph of his grandmother taken, he said in the mid-nineteenth century, an early example of portrait photography and one taken, of course, when the idea of jet flight would have seemed sheer fantasy.

About fifteen years ago, Harry fell from the roof whilst helping with repairs and he has had difficulty in walking ever since. This, however, has not dampened his spirit and the place was in 'very tidy' condition and I was met with short shrift when I tentatively suggested that he might put his feet up a bit more. He genuinely enjoyed talking about times past and we had a fascinating hour or two chatting in the sunlit farmyard. He not only remembered the Vampire but also the wartime crash of a German aircraft near Buckley. (Harry vividly described the crackling sound of this German aircraft burning as it plunged to earth. The three crew members baled out, one landing in Nerquis.)

He then directed me to Ty'n Rhyn, where the present owner Mr J Gerrard, showed me the site of the Vampire crash and allowed me to make a search. This, nevertheless, proved fruitless. The ground has been levelled and most returns on my metal detector were from old chain links and other assorted farmyard detritus. One tiny piece of alloy came to light, crumbling into greenish-white powder associated with aluminium that has spent many years underground.

The lack of physical evidence did not really surprise me. The engine and main wreckage was removed at the time and the wood, which formed much of the Vampire's construction, must have long since rotted away.

***Baltimore 1 AG689, Empire Central Flying School, Hullavington, flying from Rednal, crashed 16th September 1944 at Ledmore Hall.***

**Crash site map number 15  Map reference 126/371257**

Apart from the technical aspect, most parts of this book end in the tragedy of young lives lost serving their country in time of war and the distress of those left grieving over husbands, brothers and sons.

The loss in this chapter is no more than many others, for a Wing Commander's death is, surely, no greater deprivation to his loved ones than that of an AC2. Nevertheless, this account provides greater interest than most to the aviation historian for it involves several strands of unusual circumstance which come together on a fateful September day in 1944.

They involve a brilliant young bomber pilot and leader, a unit which had already become a by-word for excellence throughout the Allied air forces and an aircraft which, it is believed, was one of only two to crash in this country.

THE UNIT

The Central Flying School was established at Upavon, Wiltshire, in 1912. Its initial task was to train pilots for the RFC, Royal Navy and, after April 1918, the Royal Air Force. Such was its reputation that many foreign air forces based their own methods on those taught at the CFS. Not that everything was done to a rigid regime. In the twenties, before instruction began each morning, there was what was known as the 'Instructor's Ten Minutes'. This was, ostensibly, for the instructors to test the aircraft prior to the day's work, but usually developed into a period when the staff let off steam and aerobatics were carried out at below roof-top level. The authorities turned a blind eye to this practice.

When other Flying Training Schools were set up, the CFS became a school for instructors rather than pilots. It remained so until 1942 when it was felt that, to utilise the vast experience built up by the Empire Air Training Scheme, a new unit should be formed where instructors were not so much trained but given the opportunity to pool their knowledge and pass the results on to the Air Ministry and training establishments.

Only flight lieutentants and above, with 1,000 hours' flying experience, were selected and these included officers from the RAF, RN, US, SAAF, NZ, Australian, Rhodesian and even the Chinese Air Force. The courses lasted for thirteen weeks. To accommodate the multiplicity of aircraft types, a move was made to Hullavington, near Chippenham. (This was, in any case, a much more up-to-date airfield). Here, with such a wide variety of aircraft at their disposal, they were able to gain invaluable experience.

**A wide selection of 'kites' at the Empire Central Flying School.**

There were three flying units at this, now renamed, Empire Central Flying School: the Handling Flight, which prepared Pilots' Notes for new aircraft entering service, the Examining Flight which re-categorised flying instructors at flying schools and the Research Flight which investigated the various problems connected with flying training in general.

During the courses the students would visit a number of operational and training units, to acquaint themselves with the various squadrons' requirements and the training units' ability to fulfil them.

## THE AIRCRAFT

In 1939 the Glen L Martin Co of Baltimore, Maryland, produced a twin-engined light bomber, the Type 167. This failed to obtain a USAAF contract but, as the 157F, was purchased by the French government. Only a few had been delivered before the downfall of France, the remainder being supplied to the RAF and given the name Maryland. Sent by sea to the UK, all but a few were despatched to the Middle East.

**Martin Baltimore MkV.**

The Maryland was superior to the Blenheim then in use and was liked by its crews for its pleasant handling characteristics. The main drawback seems to have been that crew members were isolated from each other by bulkheads across the fuselage so that, after two hundred and fifty five had been delivered, a redesign was thought necessary.

A deeper fuselage rectified the crew communication problem while Wright Cyclone engines of 1660 hp gave it a much improved performance. With up to twelve machine guns and a bomb load of 2,000 lbs the Baltimore, as the new design was named, was an efficient light bomber, although some pilots felt that it lacked the finesse of its predecessor. In addition, the Wright engines proved more troublesome in the desert than the Pratt and Whitneys of the Maryland.

The first order for Baltimores was for four hundred machines; of these forty one were lost at sea when ships carrying them were sunk and a further two crashed before delivery.

The fourth and fifth aircraft of this first batch were AG689 and AG690, both of which were ultimately to serve at the ECFS.

AG689 was delivered to the RAF on the 4th October 1941 and taken on charge by the Directorate of Technical Development. Before testing at the Royal Aircraft Establishment, Farnborough it was despatched on the first of three lengthy visits to Cuncliffe-Owen Aircraft Co. Ltd., apparently for modifications.

After six months at RAE, a short stint at ECFS was followed by another six months at Cuncliffe-Owen. Eventually, on 29th April 1944 AG689 arrived back at ECFS only to be struck off charge less than five months later.

Both AG689 and AG690 were used to transport crews on their various unit visits.

The Operations Records Book for the month of September 1944 shows much movement of senior personnel on various duties, the greater space being reserved for the visit of King Peter of Yugoslavia, on the 28th September. Only one flying accident occurred which, unfortunately, claimed the lives of two senior officers.

## SEPTEMBER SIXTEENTH 1944

On this day a number of visits were planned for No 9 course at Hullavington. Five course members were to go to No 61 OTU

Rednal, near Oswestry, where Spitfire pilots received their final training.

The course members concerned were:

WING COMMANDER D.S. WILKERSON, DSO DFC (RAF)
LIEUTENANT COMMANDER A. PACKARD (US Navy)
SQUADRON LEADER F.W. WESTLEY, AFC (RAF)
SQUADRON LEADER JEFFERY (RCAF)
MAJOR J.W. CROSS (SAAF)

Whether they were to visit another unit on completion of their inspection at Rednal, or return directly to Hullavington, the records do not show.

They took off from Hullavington, with Wing Commander Wilkerson at the controls (although documentary evidence of this is not flawless.) On completion of their visit, however, Squadron Leader Westley was in the pilot's seat for the next leg of the flight.

The aircraft took off quite normally, probably from runway 16, but, as it began its turn away from Rednal, the Baltimore went out of control, crashing into Long Cover, a wooded area in the grounds of Ledmore Hall, south of the airfield. The aircraft caught fire and was destroyed. Two of those on board, Wing Commander Wilkerson and Major Cross were killed when the underside of the aircraft was ripped out by the trees, their bodies falling near the road. The operating crew members, seated higher in the aircraft, survived and were helped to safety. Squadron Leader Westley was taken to Copthorne Military Hospital, Shrewsbury, whilst Lieutenant Commander Packard was transferred from the Station Sick Quarters to No 68 US General Hospital. Squadron Leader Jeffery's injuries did not warrant hospital treatment.

Although preliminary investigation seemed to indicate structural failure, the evidence of the pilot soon pinpointed the cause. Squadron Leader Westley, an experienced pilot with over 4.500 flying hours to his credit, was able to clearly describe the sequence of events leading up to the crash. It appears that, as he began his turn away from the airfield after take off, rudder control was lost and the pilot could not keep the nose of the aircraft from dropping.

The Accident Investigation Branch, looking closely at the tail assembly, found the locking mechanism (which prevents the rudder from flapping around whilst the aircraft is parked) still partially locked, thus preventing full movement. They concluded that the accident was caused by a damaged rudder locking device, responsibility being attributed to 'personnel inexperienced in handling Baltimore aircraft'. Both AOC and AOC in C agreed with this conclusion.

This is the sum total of information readily available from the Public Record Office but, before jumping to the conclusion that the ground crew failed to service the aircraft properly, let us look at control locks.

Most aircraft of this period used locks which were little more than two pieces of wood clamped on either side of the control surfaces. Long red streamers attached to these simple but effective devices made their presence obvious. The controls would be immovable should the pilot attempt to use them with the locks in position. In any case, the pilots' pre-flight 'walk around' included a check to ensure that the locks were removed. It appears that the Baltimore incorporated more sophisticated internal locks operated by the pilot and these should have been safer.

So, did the pilot fail to unlock the controls? Most unlikely, as, presumably, all control surfaces would have been affected and any pilot, especially one of Squadron Leader Westley's experience, would have checked control movement as 'Full and Free' before leaving the ground. Or could it be possible that, after unlocking, previous damage caused the rudder to jam? Perhaps the answer lies somewhere in the AIB files but it is more likely that no one really knows for sure.

## THE BOMBER LEADER

A minor road meanders through the Shropshire countryside south of the village of Haughton. Alongside the road, on the edge of a wood, a finely carved wooden cross commemorates the crash of Baltimore AG689.

This cross was made and erected by Hugh Cawdron, a close friend of Wing Commander David Wilkerson DSO DFC, one of those who died. Mr Cawdron had known David since the age of seven when Hugh joined the Epping Forest Cub pack. David was, he says, an inspired scout leader and he maintained a close friendship with him from that time to the fateful day, some eight years later, when David and his companion, Major Cross, died.

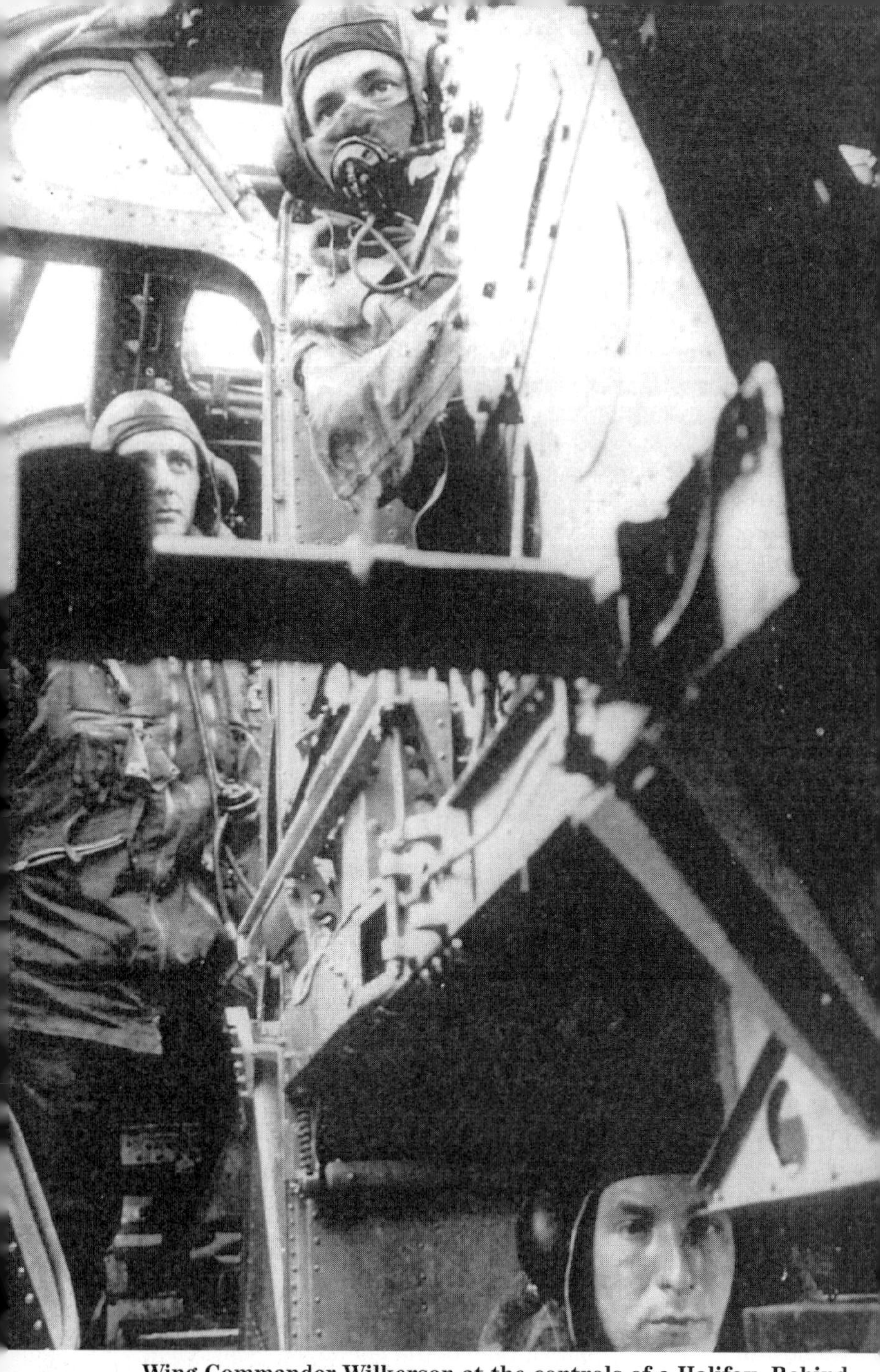

**Wing Commander Wilkerson at the controls of a Halifax. Behind him is the flight engineer and below the wireless operator.**

Hugh Cawdron has placed the memorial on the crash site, with the generous gift of land by Mrs Black of Tedsmore Hall. Unlike most memorials it has not been erected by younger researchers or well-meaning strangers, but as a tribute by an individual to a personal friend.

Hugh Cawdron has written an 'Appreciation' of the life of David Wilkerson which shows that the leadership, so evident in the Scouts, continued throughout his subsequent career. It is, perhaps, not surprising that, although most people have heard in some detail of Gibson and Cheshire etc, there were many other great wartime leaders who remain unknown even by those of us who like to think ourselves well informed on such matters.

David Wilkerson, born in London in May 1917, joined the RAFVR on 20th January 1940. His initial flying training took place at No 1 Elementary FTS Hatfield, on Tiger Moth biplanes. After a short period at Ternhill, piloting the twin-engined Anson, he was despatched across the Atlantic to continue his training at Moose Jaw, Saskatchewan. On 31st January 1941, after one hundred and twelve flying hours, David Wilkerson became both a qualified pilot and a Sergeant in the RAF.

On returning to the UK his Conversion Course at No 10 OTU Abingdon was followed by a posting to 58 Squadron, Linton-on-Ouse. Here he flew Whitley bombers, completing his first operation on 28th May.

Shortly afterwards he was posted to 35 squadron, also at Linton and continued his operational flying on Halifaxes, in attacks on various German targets including Duisburg, Essen, Hanover and Kiel. An entry from 35 squadron ORB for the Hanover raid reads as follows:

> *'Ten tenths cloud over English coast and Channel. Actual target not identified. One stick of bombs was dropped onto target area from ten thousand feet. Aircraft attacked by one and possibly two, Heinkel 113s and badly damaged by cannon fire. Starboard outer engine was hit and stopped. Controls shot through and partially jammed. Rear gunner sustained injuries as a result of the encounter but continued to fire and caused enemy to break off attacks. Aircraft returned to Bircham Newton where it crash landed'.*

Reference to the Heinkel 113 must have been a mistaken identification. The He 110D first flew in 1938 and a batch of

**Wing Commander Wilkerson, when a Flying Officer and an instructor with 35 Squadron Conversion Flight.**

twelve were formed into a unit at the factory for use by test pilots. For propaganda purposes they were painted with false unit markings, lined up for photographs and given the spurious designation He113. Those reported in action were most likely BF109s.

By now a Pilot Officer, David Wilkerson was in B Flight of 35 squadron (the Flight Commander being Flight Lieutenant Leonard Cheshire). Here he continued to notch up operations, including a number of visits to the French seaport of Brest where the seemingly indestructible German warships Scharnhorst and Gneisnau continued to pose a worrying threat to Allied shipping.

Friday 13th March 1942 proved lucky in David's calendar for, having completed twenty seven sorties, he was awarded the DFC on that day. The citation makes special mention of his determination and coolness in the operations over Brest.

He then went on to spend a number of months as an

*Inscription:*

**WING COMMANDER D. S. S. WILKERSON DSO., DFC., RAFVR**
**DIED HERE FOR HIS COUNTRY ON 16 SEPTEMBER 1944 AGED 27 YEARS**

**A survivor of 46 hazardous operations against the enemy as pilot of a Halifax bomber, he was tragically killed when travelling as passenger in a Baltimore aircraft on a domestic flight which crashed into this hillside, after taking off from Rednal airfield. He was an inspired leader who possessed the qualities of humanity, good humour and understanding, which endeared him to everybody who had the privilege of knowing him. The United States Air Force posthumously awarded him the Silver Star for Gallantry.**

**HUGH CAWDRON MADE AND ERECTED THIS CROSS IN MEMORY OF HIS FRIEND AND BROTHER SCOUT.**

instructor, passing on the skills he had acquired in action to trainees coming from OTUs. Eventually he became the Training Inspector for No 41 Base.

By this time David Wilkerson was a Wing Commander and his Commanding Officer again Leonard Cheshire, by now a Group Captain.

On 14th November 1943 David returned to his old squadron, No 51, at Snaith, where he assumed vice command. He wasted no time, involving himself once more in the bomber war by taking part in two days' intensive training, followed immediately by an attack on Mannheim. Four nights later, during an attack on Berlin, two 51 squadron aircraft were shot down, including that of the CO. Wing Commander Wilkerson thus became the Commanding Officer.

In mid-January 1944 David Wilkerson became the CO of a newly formed squadron, No 578, the nucleus of which was taken from 51 squadron. In February the new squadron moved to Burn and continued operations against the enemy until its disbandment in 1945. During this period the only VC awarded to a Halifax crew member went to Pilot Officer C J Barton who brought back his badly damaged aircraft from the disastrous Nuremburg raid, allowing his crew to escape by parachute. Pilot Officer Barton was killed in the subsequent crash landing.

In May 1944, David's work and achievements were officially recognised with the award of the DSO. Hugh Cawdron's Appreciation contains comments by many ex-crew members of 578 squadron, all of which confirm his almost legendary leadership; as Flight Lieutenant R Horton DFC put it, 'Wilkie had a gift of leadership and the ability to use it. Most of the squadron would have preferred death than to appear dishonourable in his eyes'.

After forty six operations against the enemy David Wilkerson was, on 28th August 1944, posted, as one of forty-five officers, onto No 9 course at ECFS Hullavington. At the time of his death he was, incredibly, just twenty seven years old and this remarkable young man was buried near Burn, at Selby Town Cemetery. In November 1944 he was posthumously awarded the Silver Star by the USAAF for gallantry in action and for his 'inspiration to fellow fliers'.

Of his fellow course member, Major James Cross of the South African Air Force, little is known. At the time of his death he was thirty-two years old, his home was in Worcester, Cape Province and he is buried in Blacon Cemetery, Chester.

The memorial cross is placed where the Baltimore crashed but on no account should any attempt be made to look for fragments in this wood. The land is strictly private and, as the location is already precisely mapped, it would serve no useful purpose to venture further.

**Remains of AG689 discovered at the time when the memorial was erected.**

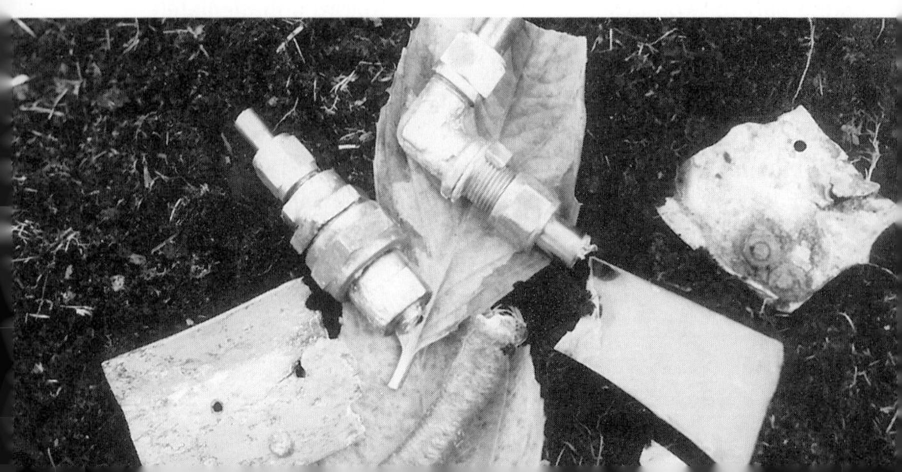

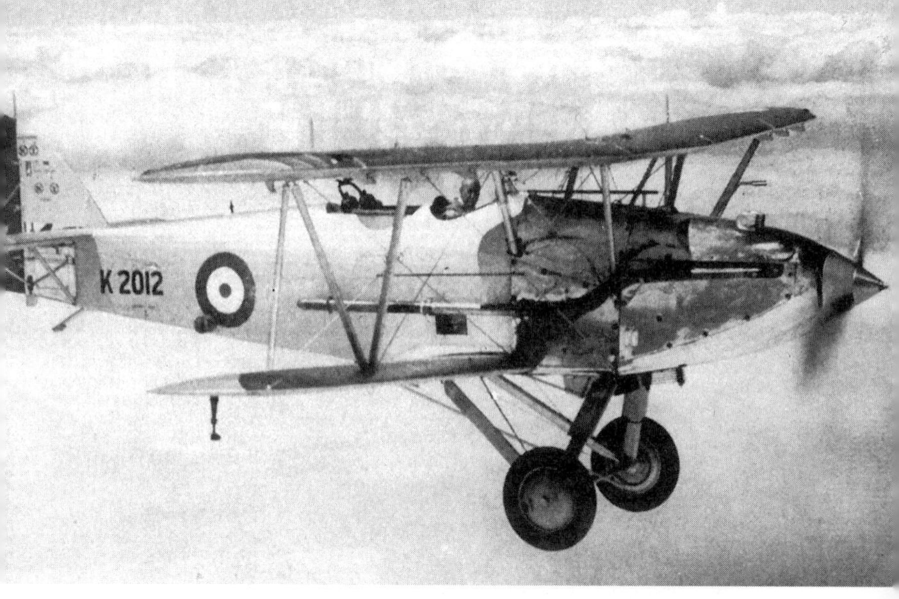


***Audax K7435, No.11 Flying Training School, Shawbury, on an air firing exercise, crashed 12th October 1938 at Forton Heath.***

**Crash site map number 16 Map reference 126/438172**

The Hawker Hart was built, to Air Ministry specification 12/26, as the RAF's standard light bomber. Powered by a Rolls-Royce Kestrel 525 hp in-line engine, it carried a 500 lb bomb load over a range of 470 miles at a maximum speed of 184 mph. Although this may seem almost pedestrian by today's standards, in 1928 it was brisk enough to elude all but the best fighters of the period.

So efficient was the Hart that it was used in most roles; the multi-role aircraft of its day. Rather than being allocated a Mark number, as was done with aircraft in WW2, each variant was given a separate identity. Thus the Hind, Hardy, Demon, Osprey, Hector and Audax (Audax: [latin] Bold, as in audacious).

Crews that worked on these aircraft certainly knew the difference between them but to others less versed in such esoteric points as exhaust pipe lengths, tyre dimensions, bomb racks etc they were often just known collectively as 'Hart variants'.

Used for Army Co-operation, the Audax had, apart from other differences, a hook pivoted on the undercarriage spreader bar, for picking up messages in flight. Thus, to most ground crews, the Audax became the 'Art with an 'ook!

**A Hawker Audax at 11 FTS.**

Production of the Audax totalled 624 which, apart from those built by the parent company, were constructed by Gloster, Bristol, Westland and Avro. The Audax served with distinction throughout the 1930s, particularly in India and the Middle East. In 1941 they acquitted themselves well as part of a scratch force which defended RAF Habbaniya, Iraq, during the rebellion when forces, led by Raschid Ali attempted to capture the base.

By 1937 the Audax, with a downrated Kestrel engine, was relegated to a training role, having been replaced in front-line squadrons by the Hector.

K7435, delivered to the RAF in December 1936 was allocated, in mid-1937, to 148 squadron, (newly reformed at Scampton, having been disbanded in 1919). Later that year, 148 sqn was re-equipped with Vickers Wellesleys, its Audax aircraft passing to No 11 FTS at Shawbury.

There, K7435 had an eventful life, colliding with K7501 during formation flying practice and, after repair, collapsing its undercarriage on the runway during night flying at Wittering in March 1938. Repaired again, it was back in service for another six months before wrecking itself so comprehensively that even the skilled engineering staff at Shawbury were unable to put it together again.

On the morning of Tuesday 12th October 1938, Acting Pilot Officer J D Withers in K7435, accompanied by another Audax,

took-off from Shawbury on an air firing exercise. Over the Shropshire countryside they made camera gun attacks on a drogue target towed by another aircraft, probably a Fairey Gordon.

During a diving attack Pilot Officer Withers found himself unable to control the aircraft and, after struggling with the controls for some seconds, the ground getting ever closer, took to his parachute. Having little time in the air to correct his descent, the pilot could not avoid a small copse and so found himself suspended by his parachute lines in the branches of a large tree. This tree overhung a cottage which itself was near the banks of the flooded river Perry, a tributary of the Severn. Although some of the lower branches of the tree had to be sawn off to release him, the pilot, apart from a few bruises, was little the worse for wear.

The other Audax pilot, observing these events, landed in a field nearby. Pilot Officer Withers, doubtless remembering the old adage about remounting your horse immediately after a spill, took over the controls and within minutes they were back on the tarmac at Shawbury.

Meanwhile K7435, having gone into a near vertical dive, crashed into a field near the village of Fitz. Only a tangled mass of wreckage remained after the fuel tanks had exploded and the engine buried itself some six feet into the ground.

Police Sergeants McPherson and Hanwood with PC Masters from Montford Bridge, together with RAF personnel, mounted guard over the wreckage which was fenced off pending investigation.

As is usual in such circumstances, a Court of Inquiry was

**The *Border Counties Advertizer* in its issue of 13th October, 1938, published a picture of the crash along with the following caption: 'All that was left of a Hawker Audax light bomber which dived out of control into a field near Fitz yeaterday (Tuesday) morning. The pilot made a miraculous escape by parachute'.**

convened to establish the cause of the accident. Study of the relevant documents reveal that Acting Pilot Officer J D G Withers was on a Short Service Commission. Trained at Hamble, near Southampton, he was awarded his Wings on 20th August 1938, just two months before the crash. He had flown a total of fifty one hours dual and sixty five solo, including twenty four and twenty respectively on the Audax. Pilot Officer Withers was later promoted to Flight Lieutenant and awarded the DFC. He was killed in action on 22nd June 1941whilst flying Hampdens with No. 83 Squadron.

It was determined that the crash was caused by the failure of the starboard aileron. Disciplinary action was taken against two airmen found to be responsible for servicing the aircraft.

* * * * * *

My friend and colleague Hedley Richards has given me enormous help in researching crash sites in Shropshire. He has scoured the local archives for many years, searching for details of pre-war accidents and K7435 has occupied his attention for some time now. The contemporary newspapers reported the

**A metal detector search identified the crash site.**

event but pinpointing the exact location seemed an almost impossible task.

I must admit that I gave him little encouragement, viewing the chances of finding any remains of a biplane which had crashed some sixty years earlier as virtually nil. I had thought that an Audax with engine trouble, or whatever, would make an almost gentle crash-landing and that the remains would be removed practically intact.

Early 1998 proved to be a breakthrough for Hedley. He discovered that the aircraft had been abandoned because of control failure, had crashed heavily and burnt out, thus greatly improving our chances of finding some fragments. After speaking to a number of local farmers, Hedley eventually found one who was able to point out the exact spot where the Audax crashed.

Hedley's metal detector search and our subsequent visit together, revealed a large number of items only a couple of inches below the surface, the field not having been ploughed. One, a stainless steel spar connector, bore the inspection mark R3. This had me baffled for a moment. The factory stamp for Avro is R3, which would be unusual on a Hawker product. Referring to my 'bible' (*Aircraft of the RAF since 1918* by O Thetford) on these matters, it was interesting to find, however, that 287 Audax aircraft were built by Avro and that K7435 was one of these.

The find of the spar connector, plus other pieces, with inspectors' stamps was staggering; though most aircraft parts are marked, to discover fragments from a pre-war biplane at a previously unresearched site was extremely lucky.

Finally, showing that F1180 are not an infallible source of information, the pilot's experience was shown as only one month and the location of the crash as Acton Heath. Pilot Officer Withers' experience was, in fact, nearly double that quoted while the OS map shows the area as Forton Heath.

**Fragments including part o the trim tab wheel, stainless steel connector, fuel pipe and cowling vent.**

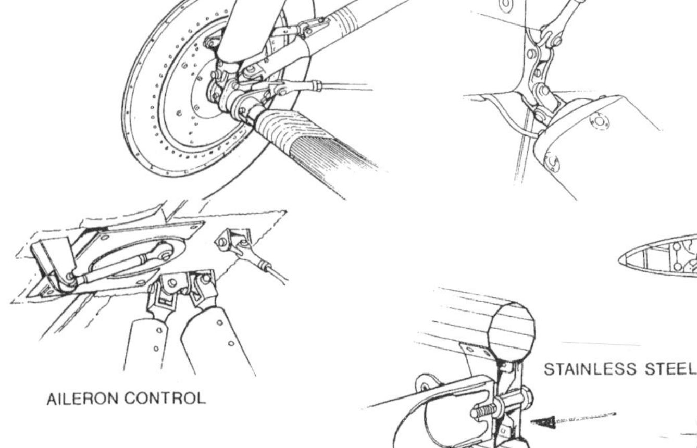

***Spitfire MkIIA P7963, No 61 Operational Training Unit, Rednal, flying practice, crashed 8th September 1942 at Lower Haughton Farm.***

**Crash site map number 17 Map reference 126/372271**

The fate of the first Spitfire to leave the Castle Bromwich factory is recorded in another chapter in this book. Number four hundred and twelve on the production line of this first contract was P7963. It was initially delivered to No 54 Squadron, on 4th February 1941, then passed to another fighter unit, No 331 (Czech) Squadron. P7963 finally spent its remaining nineteen months at two OTUs, numbers 58 and 61 and was struck off charge on 10th September 1942.

Stanley Lister was born in Folkestone in 1921 and, in the 1930s, worked in the Royal Engineers Survey Department, Shorncliffe. In 1939, together with his brother, he joined the Territorial Army and at one time was assigned to airfield defence at RAF Hawkinge. This posting no doubt increased his already stated desire to become a pilot. There were, however, a number of frustrations before he was finally accepted for flying training.

Stanley Lister began his flying at Number 1 EFTS, Hatfield, before being sent by sea to continue his training in Canada. There, at the evocatively named Swiftcurrent air base, he flew Tiger Moth biplanes before graduating, getting both his 'wings' and his Sergeants stripes on the ubiquitous North American Harvard. Another sea journey across the Atlantic brought him back to Britain to complete his training at 61 OTU Rednal, near Oswestry.

Rednal airfield was opened in 1942 and closed just three years later. Here, during this period, thousands of pilots received their operational training on Spitfires and Mustangs.

The massive torque reaction caused by the rotation of the propeller on powerful single engined aircraft also made the rear fuselage attempt to rotate. This had to be countered by the pilot at an early stage if an uncontrollable swing, usually becoming worse after the aircraft had left the ground, was to be avoided. It was this swing which caused the crash of P7963 and the death of Sgt Lister.

On 8th September 1942, Sgt Lister began his take-off on runway 16. As the aircraft left the ground, the swing which had already developed became uncontrollable and the aircraft crashed through the roof of an old building at Haughton Farm, on the airfield perimeter. The wings sheared off and the fuselage came to rest in the cobbled yard of the farm. These events were observed from the Watch Office so both fire tender and ambulance were quickly on the scene. There was no fire and Sgt Lister was carefully removed from the wreckage but, despite the efforts of the medical personnel, he died in the farmyard.

Roger Hampson was five

**Sergeant S. P. Lister**

IN MEMORY
OF
SERGEANT PILOT S. P. LISTER R. A. F.
BORN: 3rd NOVEMBER 1921
DIED: 8th SEPTEMBER 1942
"THERE IS NO GREATER LOVE THAN THIS, THAT SOMEONE SHOULD LAY DOWN HIS LIFE FOR HIS FRIENDS."

**Lower Haughton Farm, crash site in the foreground.**

years old on that fateful day and, from the safety of the farmhouse door where he had been told to stand, watched his father take the horses from an adjacent brick building. Seconds later the aircraft hit this building, the fuselage skidding across the yard just feet away from the terrified child. Roger recalled his mother rushing out to bring him back indoors while 100 octane petrol spilled across the yard and into the drains. Luckily there was no fire.

This site has been thoroughly researched by Mike Davies of Shrewsbury and others; a plaque, in memory of the pilot, has been fixed to the wall of the building near the spot where Sgt Lister died.

Despite the many visitors who must have come to Haughton Farm, Mr Hampson showed no sign of impatience at the arrival of yet another. Indeed, he was only too willing to recount the events which are indelibly imprinted on his memory. The farm lies within the boundary of the old airfield. A brick pill box still

Early Mark Spitfires with twin-bladed wooden propellers. Note the mascot lined up for inspection and looking very proud.

**Roger Hampson holding a part of the wooden propeller blade of P7963 on the spot where it was discovered over 50 years ago.**

stands at the farm gate and Roger well remembers going inside, with the troops, to look at the guns. The sound of aircraft was, of course, ever present at that time and, had he disobeyed his father's instructions, it is unlikely that he would have survived. As it was, it was lucky that the aircraft came to rest where it did, he said, because the airfield petrol installation lay just a few hundred yards further on.

Roger showed me where he was standing on 8th September 1942 and pointed to the repairs in the outbuilding roof and wall though now, after fifty or so years, they are beginning to blend in with the old structure. The yard is quite small so the horrific events which unfolded within its narrow confines must have been both frightening and exciting to a small child. The only piece of wreckage remaining is a fragment of a wooden propeller blade which Roger brought out to be photographed.

It was gratifying to find that Sgt Lister's sacrifice had not been forgotten in this quiet Shropshire farmyard.

Much of Rednal aerodrome can still be seen today, as a public road utilises part of a runway. The Watch Office stands in a cornfield and it takes but a little leap of the imagination to feel the reverberations as Merlin engines echo around the now desolate buildings.

***Spitfire MkIIA P7280, No 61 Operational Training Unit, Rednal, formation practice, crashed 15th September 1944 at Crickheath Farm.***

**Crash site map number 18        Map reference 126/302233**

Even before the start of the Second World War it was realised that the production capability of the Supermarine works at Southampton could not keep pace with the RAF's requirements for the Spitfire. The industry, as related elsewhere in this volume, was not as well geared up to mass-production as were car factories.

Lord Nuffield, head of the Morris Motors concern, was approached with a view to setting up a new factory which could produce the Spitfire in the numbers needed. For various reasons, both political and industrial, the site chosen was at Castle Bromwich, Birmingham.

The initial contract placed was for one thousand Mark 11A Spitfires, the first, P7280, being delivered on 27th June 1940.

The Mark 11A used the Merlin X11 engine, running on 100 octane fuel, which gave improved performance. (Without higher octane fuels, development of the Merlin engine throughout the rest of the war would have been impossible.) Other modifications were minor, indeed, the new mark number was of use mainly as a means of differentiation between Castle Bromwich and Southampton built Spitfires to facilitate spares ordering. The 'A' suffix relates to the wing layout; in this case one with four 0.303 inch machine guns in each wing.

The immediate area around every war-time airfield became, unfortunately, the graveyard of many aircraft. Engine failure or uncontrolled swing on take-off are phenomena virtually unknown with today's modern aircraft, but all too common then.

Formation flying also claimed many a life, as wing-men struggled to control speed and altitude in an effort to stay well tucked into the leader. When cloud is encountered, leaders must quickly decide whether it is thin enough to stay in tight

**Early Spitfire cockpit.**

Spitfire production in full swing at the Castle Bromwich factory.

Alex Henshaw, chief test pilot at Castle Bromwich in deep conversation with Winston Churchill.

The Spitfire's power plant, the Rolls-Royce Merlin.

formation or, if contact is lost, scatter to a pre-determined plan. In hostile skies it is sometimes preferable to keep the aircraft together and, no doubt, cloud was frequently flown through on a wing and a prayer. In such conditions pilots must have an acute awareness of space and time, together with complete confidence in their instruments.

P7280, first to leave the Castle Bromwich factory, arrived at the Boscombe Down experimental establishment on 27th June 1940 where it was tested in comparison with a Mark 1 Spitfire. P7280 had improved climb and ceiling but was less stable in the climb; whether this slight instability had any bearing on its final demise is unknown. After modifications at Air Service Training it returned to Boscombe for diving tests with weighted elevator

**Testing the undercarriage of a MkV at Castle Bromwich.**

**A colleague takes a break at the crash site. Searching had to take place in the 'window of opportunity' between harvesting and re-seeding.**

controls and also trials of a new sliding cockpit hood which gave better visibility. On 2nd July 1943 P7280 was 'retired' to 61 OTU Rednal for use as an operational trainer.

F Sgt G L Smith was an experienced pilot with four hundred and forty seven hours in his flying log book. The date of his initial training is unsure but it is known that he was flying in 1942, or even earlier. In the period between then and his arriving at Rednal for training on the Spitfire in August 1944, the records make it clear that he had done no flying in cloud for nearly two years. Without checking the ORBs of numerous unspecified units, it can only be surmised that the most likely duty involving flying only Visual Meteorological Conditions, was ferrying – but this can only be conjecture. Nevertheless, F Sgt Smith was a course member at 61 OTU and had certainly reached the formation flying stage of training.

On 15th September 1944, three Spitfires took off for formation flying practice, with F Sgt Smith in P7280.

At Lower Morton Farm John Edwards, aged 16, heard the sound of an aircraft engine misfiring, typical of a Rolls-Royce Merlin engine when throttled back. On rushing outside he saw a

Spitfire circle, lose height and, finally dive into an adjacent field. Accompanied by a workmate he ran across to the wreckage and found the pilot slumped over the controls, apparently unconscious. Although fearful that the aircraft would catch fire they bravely tried to free him. Unable to release the harness, they hacked through the shoulder straps with a penknife, only to find the pilot trapped by his legs, despite all their efforts to extract him.

There was nothing they could do but anxiously await the arrival of the emergency services. After that they were kept away from the wreckage, although the salvage team often came to the farm for water etc.

A lady living at the opposite end of the field well remembers standing on the five-barred gate as a girl, seeing the tail of the aircraft in the distance and, later, the wreckage being carted away through the same gate.

* * * * *

THE COURT OF INQUIRIES' INVESTIGATION

This revealed that when the formation entered cloud P7280, for reasons unknown, left the formation, appeared to enter a spin and crash. The pilot had obviously been unable to maintain station in cloud and lost control.

On looking at the pilot's records, it soon transpired that F Sgt Smith had not taken part in formation flying for some fourteen months and, as stated earlier, had no recent experience of flying in cloud. The C of I found that the Flight Commander had authorised the flight without first making himself aware of these facts and ensuring that the pilot was capable. The AOC recommended disciplinary action to be taken against the Flt Cdr and the AOC in C concurred.

* * * * *

The aircraft crashed in a field on Crickheath Farm. It is now much larger than in 1944, as hedges have been removed. Despite this, because its closeness to a patch of boggy ground, John Edwards was able to pinpoint the location.

Shortly before my visit a deep search of the area had been made by a local group, so only tiny fragments of this sad episode were to be found.

***Anson 1 K6248, No.2 School of Air Navigation, Shawbury, unauthorised landing practice, crashed 21st March 1941 at Hawkswood Farm.***

**Crash site map number 19 Map reference 126/370299**

In another chapter I remark on the tendency for the Accident Investigation Branch to go beyond their remit in investigating the evidence. They often make reference to possible crew negligence, or of crews disregarding instructions, when they cannot possibly have anything concrete on which to base these assumptions.

The accident reports are not for the general public but must, if released, cause relatives pain and even anger. This habit of the AIB still persists, I believe, but families of dead crew members blamed for 'gross negligence' have made their worries public, so perhaps this climate will soon change.

The crash of Anson K 6248 is almost a reversal of the old policy; the crew were, it was said, performing 'unauthorised' manoevres, but they were not greatly censured. Did the fact that the pilot was a pre-war officer trained at Cranwell have any bearing on the case? Perhaps it is invidious to ask, but it is always interesting to read the official documents and compare them with eye-witness reports. The statements made by different witnesses on the ground, are, in any case often at variance with each other. No two people seem to see the same event similarly. Fred Stockton played football for the nearby Frankton team whenever he had the opportunity, but 21st March 1941 was a working day for him, at Hawkswood Farm, near Oswestry. He emerged from the barn just before eleven in the morning, on hearing the tortured sound of aircraft engines being revved up. A small twin-engined aeroplane was circling at low level, climbing, diving and manoeuvring – 'showing off a bit', thought Fred.

Suddenly, the aircraft dived towards the trees behind the farmhouse and, in climbing sharply away, the tail struck the tops of the trees, breaking off. The aircraft plummeted to the ground, killing all those on board. A fire engine from Ellesmere arrived, but nothing could be done for men or machine.

Flying Officer E W Padfield joined the RAF before the outbreak of war and attended the prestigious RAF College at Cranwell where, on 6th April 1939, he qualified as a Pilot Officer (General Duties Branch).

By the time he took up his appointment as a Staff pilot, at No 2 School of Air Navigation, he had over two hundred flying hours to his credit and, by 21st March 1941, had accumulated a further one hundred and twenty six hours solo on the Anson. On that morning, with it is believed, a number of trainee navigators on board, he took off on a navigation practice detail. That is the total positive information available, for soon after at 11.05 am, Flying Officer Padfield and his charges were all dead.

A check of the Air Ministry Form 1180 (Accident Report) reveals that Flying Officer Padfield's C.O. was unsure of the reason for this disaster. He was of the opinion that the pilot, on attempting a forced landing and making an overshoot, was too late in opening the throttles and that the tail struck a tree, causing the aircraft to crash.

The C of I which followed, concluded that the aircraft hit a tree whilst carrying out an 'unauthorised' precautionary landing practice. How they knew this is rather baffling; the aircraft crashed away from the airfield and, if unauthorised, those in authority would not have known about it.

The AOC at the time also appeared uncertain. He thought the evidence conflicting, but tended to support the theory that the wheels were down and that the pilot was trying to land, 'for some obscure reason'.

The Chief Inspector of Accidents agreed with the Court of Inquiry, adding that, in his opinion, the pilot also failed to appreciate the downwind direction of his dummy run.

So, why did Anson K 6248 crash? Was the pilot enjoying a

spot of low flying, his C.O., laudably, not, as they say, dropping him in it? Or was there some real emergency, making an immediate landing imperative? Perhaps the Court of Inquiry was right and Flying Officer Padfield was, indeed, practising forced landings on a navigational training flight (unlikely as it seems!).

Perhaps the answer lies in some file in the PRO, just waiting for someone to blow off the dust and reveal all. In my opinion, for what it is worth, nearly sixty years after the event and with no new evidence, the pilot, making a forced landing, practice or for real, allowed his approach speed to decay excessively and stalled into the trees.

Unfortunately, we must leave it there, otherwise we will spend all our time indoors at Kew instead of in the countryside.

Mr Faulkner, the present owner, welcomed us at Hawkswood Farm, giving us all the information he had received from the previous owner, Fred Stockton (now deceased). Mr Faulkner took us to the spot in the woods, behind the house, where the Anson crashed, but searching amongst the trees turned out to be a laborious task. It being high summer the bracken and willow herb were waist deep and, although we hacked away for a couple of hours, only minute fragments could be found. Others had searched before, but failure to find further evidence is of no consequence; the position is recorded and the main interest here lies in not where, but why the Anson crashed.

Llanbedr
and
Dolgellau

***Wellington Mk1c HX433, 1443 Ferry Flight, on a fuel consumption flight from Harwell, crashed 28th May 1942 on Mynydd Moel.***

**Crash site map number 20 Map reference 124/728138**

In the photograph above Wellington R1333, paid for by employees of the Broughton factory, is about to be 'christened' with a bottle of wine which is suspended between the propeller and the fuselage. Exactly one week later, the Luftwaffe, taking a rather jaundiced view of Broughton's activities, raided the factory and R1333 was destroyed.

The appellation 'Wimpy', given to the Wellington, had its origins in the Popeye cartoon syndicated world-wide and read by millions each day in the Daily Mirror. J Wellington Wimpy was a rather portly character known, amongst other things, for his consumption of hamburgers, a delicacy not so widespread in pre-war Britain as it is today. The Wellington aircraft is, unfortunately, unknown to most people today, whereas 'Wimpy' hamburger emporiums grace many a high street.

The Wimpy aircraft served at one time or another in twelve squadrons in the Middle East, carrying out invaluable work from bases in Malta, Egypt and later Italy. This consisted in the main, of attacks on enemy shipping in North African ports such as Benghazi and Tobruk.

It is a little known fact that the pathfinders, or target illuminators, for many of these operations were Fairey Albacore biplanes of the Fleet Air Arm, an aircraft which has sunk into even greater obscurity than most other WW II aircraft.

Despite all aircraft and engines being built to the same specification, there was often considerable difference in the performance and fuel consumption of individual machines. It was therefore essential for a fuel consumption test to be carried out before undertaking the long sea legs to Gibraltar and Malta.

At about 1200 hours on 28th May 1942 a crew of 1443 Ferry Flight, based at RAF Harwell, boarded their transport to take them to the hard standing where HX433 was parked. The Captain was Sgt W J Grant, a pilot with 143 solo flying hours to his credit, 57 of them on type. As he walked around the aircraft checking engines, undercarriage and such control surfaces as were accessible, the other crew members were busy completing their checks inside. The crew were:

| | |
|---|---|
| SGT W J GRANT | Pilot RCAF |
| SGT H L DAVIS | Pilot RCAF |
| SGT H N WILLIAMS | WOP/AG |
| SGT G D GRAHAM | Observer (Navigator) |
| SGT J I MCPOWELL | WOP/AG |
| SGT C J THOMAS | AG |

Shortly after, they taxied out and, at about 1230 hours, took off

**The northern face of Mynydd Moel.**

on a flight to check fuel consumption. (No figures were available, as the aircraft had only recently been delivered from the factory at Weybridge.)

At approximately 1430 hours HX433, having strayed some 20 degrees off course and in cloud, crashed into the northern face of Mynydd Moel, killing all those on board. Other aircraft, on the correct route, reported the weather as good.

The aircraft struck near the summit, wreckage cascading down the scree slopes.

* * * * *

I was accompanied on my journey by Matthew Rimmer. I write 'accompanied' but should really say guided, for it was through his local contacts that the site, though previously mentioned, was actually located.

If only all aviation 'enthusiasts' had this young man's dedication, the location of crash sites and their subsequent treatment would be in safer hands than is usually the case. Starting in 1992 when only fourteen, Matthew, helped by his mother Jenny, began the arduous task of tracing the relatives of many of those killed in the crash of B17 44-6005 near

Barmouth. He was also instrumental in having the permanent memorial erected near the site on 8th June 1995, the fiftieth anniversary of the crash.

The car may be parked where the road ends, at MR 124/744150, near to Bwlch Coch. Care must be taken when starting the walk to observe the footpath signs, as the path is not clearly defined and passes through private property.

Then comes the hardish walk across broken, sometimes boggy ground towards Mynydd Moel itself. Llyn Arran, shown on the map, lies in a dip and cannot be seen if on course.

**Matthew Rimmer dedicated to the location of crash sites and their subsequent treatment.**

The mountain is only about 125 feet lower than the Cader Idris massif but fear not for, although HX433 crashed only a little below the summit, the wreckage fell down its northern slopes and the remains now lie in a tumble of rocks and scree only a short way up.

Many hundreds of fragments are to be seen at the site but a word of warning: the scree is loose and quite large rocks, apparently firm footholds, can move alarmingly when stepped upon. This may start a chain reaction, making you rather glad you took advice about not venturing into the hills alone.

One piece of wreckage I uncovered was, as it clearly stated on its side, part of a Planisphere Mark 1A made by LNP & Co Ltd, ref 6B/153. (A device, apparently, for locating heavenly bodies for navigational purposes.)

***Wellington B MkX HE872, 26 Operational Training Unit, on a training exercise via Llanbedr, crashed 4th November 1943 at Ynys Gwrtheyrn.***

**Crash site map number 21** **Map reference 124/578243**

On 3rd November 1943, Sgt 'Les' Edwards and his crew of six (an additional gunner had just joined them; unnecessary on the Wellington, he would be needed when the crew later moved onto the Stirling) other NCOs took off, from 26 OTU, Little Horwood on their last solo exercise prior to posting onto a Stirling Heavy Conversion Unit. Whilst over North Wales the aircraft flew into bad weather; many years later the co-pilot Sergeant Harry George wrote his own account:

*'We were at 16000 feet when we flew into a cumulonimbus cloud and all of a sudden everything went haywire. I was pinned to the top of the aircraft by the forces that took control of us, then the aircraft started a steep dive. This was so abrupt that anything loose hurtled towards the nose and there was terrific noise from the engines as we careered downwards, still in cloud. Les Edwards and I pulled back on the stick, to no avail at first but gradually the rate of descent became more controlled. We broke cloud over the water, with*

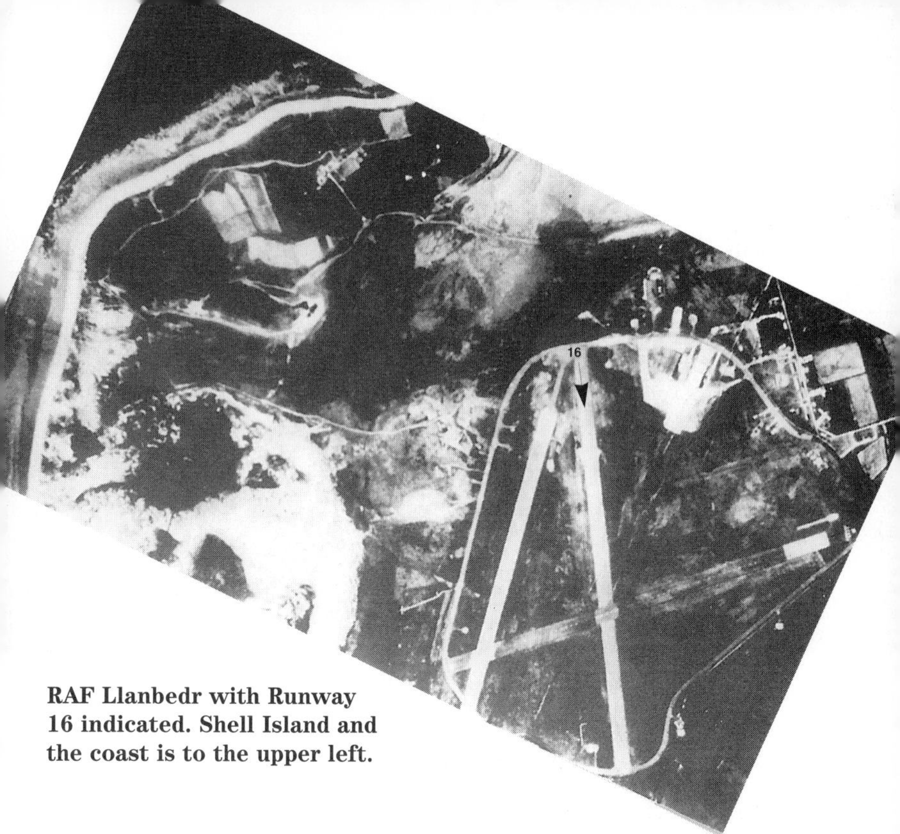


**RAF Llanbedr with Runway 16 indicated. Shell Island and the coast is to the upper left.**

*the plane still refusing to maintain height. So relieved were we that we all cried 'Ditch it Les!' but, like the ending to a bad dream, a runway appeared ahead. Still descending and, by chance, perfectly lined up, Les landed at Llanbedr aerodrome.'*

What rectification was required to HE872, after this frightening incident, is not known; the Llanbedr Operations Record Book merely notes that the aircraft had 'iced-up at 15000 feet'. Apart from a general check of the machine and the instruments in particular, it is unlikely that much work was needed.

On the following day, 4th November, Sgt Edwards decided to take HE872 on a test flight, prior to returning to 26 OTU. Sergeant George the co-pilot and 'Chick' the Australian navigator stayed behind and, in their place two Spitfire pilots from Llanbedr went along for the ride – believed to be Sergeant J. Frisby and Sergeant S. Rowan.

Just after mid-day, Les Edwards lined up the aircraft on runway one-six at Llanbedr and started his take-off run. Most of the 1400 yards of tarmac had already disappeared behind them

**HE872 crashed in the foreground near the abandoned farm building.**

but still the aircraft showed a marked reluctance to leave the ground. Eventually staggering into the air it still refused to climb and so struck rising ground, only a mile from the end of the runway.

HE872 burst into flames on impact but, with one exception, the crew struggled to safety. That exception was Sgt R Humpage, the extra gunner who had not really been needed on the flight, but who died in the flames.

Three men were injured sufficiently to be detained in Llanbedr hospital, Sgt N O'Hamley the rear gunner with head injuries. The dead gunner's body was taken back to his home town and later the co-pilot and the navigator attended his funeral at Ashton-under-Lyne. The flight duration was recorded as five minutes.

The Commanding Officer at Llanbedr noted that, on realising that the aircraft was not rising, the pilot should have throttled back and retracted the undercarriage. In this way the aircraft would at least have come to a standstill within the confines of the airfield. (Thus, by implication, the fatality could have been avoided.)

A Court of Inquiry, set up by the Station Commander revealed a whole litany of errors, although it does appear that most of these were of an administrative nature:

**Fragments of HE872 including panels, pipes, bullets and links.**

The flight was unauthorised as the pilot should have sought permission from his base at 26 OTU. HE872 had not been cleared for flight by the ground crew NCO, believed to be a Sgt O'Connor, nor had the pilot signed the appropriate Form 700, accepting the machine as serviceable. The C of I criticised Sgt Edwards' cockpit drill and, on my careful reading between the lines, seems to imply that this was the actual cause of the crash: the tail trim was wound too far forward, thus preventing effective use of the elevators.

On instructions from the AOC Sgt Edwards log book was endorsed 'Disobedience'. No mention is made in the summary of the additional and, presumably, unauthorised presence of the two Spitfire pilots.

* * * * *

With the permission of the owner, I went to the crash site which is but a few hundred yards from the deserted buildings of Ynys Gwrtheyrn. Runway 16 at Llanbedr is still in use and the white stripes marking its end can be clearly seen from the crash site. A metal detector is not needed, for the stone walls and the ground beneath them are littered with airframe fragments and exploded 0.303 inch cartridges, some of which had been fired. These must have remained in the aircraft since its last live firing practice. Unusually too, in my experience, the ammunition was new at the time, the rims stamped 1943.

Let me end with the words of Harry George, the co-pilot: 'When asked if I flew from Llanbedr, my answer is No, but I certainly landed there and Boy, were we glad to on that fateful day'.

***Wellington Mk1A N2866, No.18 Operational Training Unit, on a training exercise via Llanbedr, crashed 15th October 1941 near Llanbedr.***

**Crash site map number 22 Map reference 124/593264***

Despite my emphasis throughout this book on personally going to the location of each crash, I have included a site that I have not visited at all! (Though I have made strenuous attempts to find it.) I include it, in the remote hope that some reader may be able to tell me where the site is! It is worth recording because it involves the final demise of an aircraft, built prior to the war and which took part in one of the first daylight attacks by Bomber Command.

On 18th December 1939 twenty four Wellingtons in four groups of six aircraft were sent out to attack German warships in the region of Heligoland and Schillig Roads. At this stage of the war, crews had been briefed not to drop bombs on warships in the docks or moored alongside quays; such was the desire to avoid civilian casualties. Flak and German fighters decimated the formations and ten of the Wellingtons were shot down. The

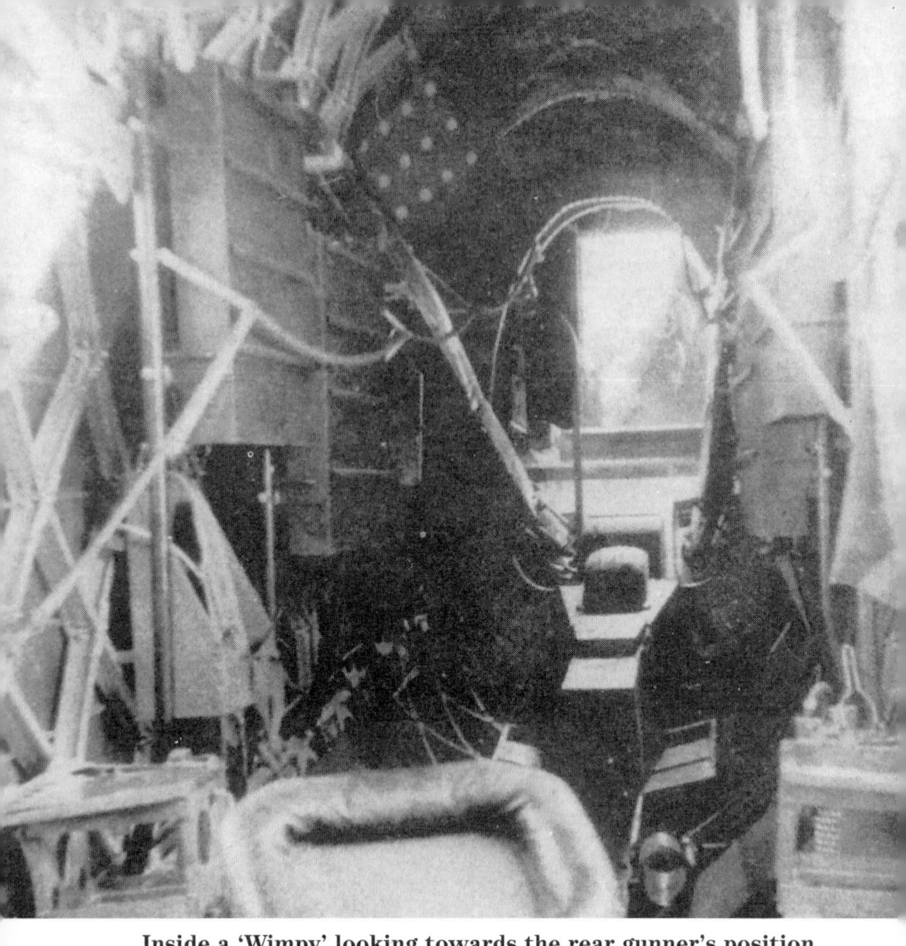

**Inside a 'Wimpy' looking towards the rear gunner's position.**

**The likely area of the crash site – but just where do you begin looking?**

illustration above is of Wellington N2871 with damage to fuselage and both wings after the raid on Wilhelmshaven. Their lack of self-sealing fuel tanks and vulnerability to beam attacks made them easy prey for the forty four Luftwaffe Messerschmitt 109 and 110s sent up to intercept them. This action, in which no ships were damaged by the attacking force, caused the whole policy of daylight bombing to be seriously questioned.

Not long after this traumatic event N2866, which took part in the action, was retired to 18 OTU Bramcote, Warwickshire, for training duties.

On 15th October 1941 the mainly Polish crew of N2866 took-off from Bramcote on a cross-country exercise. They were, if my spelling does not fail me:

| | |
|---|---|
| Pilot Officer | MENDELA |
| Flying Officer | ADRIAN |
| Flying Officer | SKUHALA |
| Sergeant | FRZEBRATOWSKA |
| Sergeant | LISZEWSKI |
| AC | JENKINS |
| AC | MOSS |

Whilst over North Wales, the old bug-bear, carburettor icing, was encountered, the port Pegasus engine, serial number 186045, failed as a result.

Although only a few miles from Llanbedr airfield the pilot thought it serious enough to attempt a forced landing on the hillside. He made a good job of it but in the process, the starboard engine, serial number 142858, caught fire. The crew were able to escape unharmed and the fire was extinguished.

The Commanding Officer decided that the pilot failed to use the hot air intake causing the engine to ice up. (This is not quite so simple as it may seem; hot air was only switched on when it was known that the icing index was high, and crews were often caught out.)

Pilot Officer Mendela had also, in the CO's view, made an error of judgement in not landing at Llanbedr.

With all this knowledge to hand, why is the location of the crash site so elusive? The Form 1180 states that N2866 landed one and a half miles east of Llanbedr. I give a map reference here, but the critical factor must be from what point is the distance measured? Without this knowledge and with no other information to hand an accurate search is impossible.

A.M. Form 1180

| D | M | Y | Unit | Group | Command |
|---|---|---|---|---|---|
| 15 | 10 | 41 | 8 O.T.U (P) | 6 | B |

| Signal No | A 788 | A : B : C | B | 1400 Duty | × [illegible] | Fire ~~in air~~ ~~or impact~~ | EXT Yes |
|---|---|---|---|---|---|---|---|
| 765c | 590 24/10 | K | I | | | Parachute Fitted | |
| A.I.B. | | — | 1 | | | Parachute Used | |
| C of I | A.315509/41 | | | Aircraft | WELLINGTON IA N.2866 | W:R:M | W |
| ~~Aerodrome~~ ~~or~~ Place | ~~Home: Foreign~~ Not on: Llanbedr (1½ m. E) | Engine | Pegasus XVIII | 1560045 / 142355 | R / R | Flotation Gear Fitted / Worked / Lives saved / A/c salved | |

E.F. (icing) ~~M.[illegible]~~ (noted) Failure of port engine due to icing — pilot flying in cold air. Force landed on hillside. Stbd. engine caught fire but was extinguished. Pilot failed to use hot air intake. O.C.:- E of J in failing to land on aerodrome.

Cause: L17 B

The Air Ministry Form 1180 setting out the briefest details of the accident. An 1180 was completed

# Mid Wales

***Wellington Mk1 L4230, No.15 Operational Training Unit, on a routine training flight from Harwell, crashed 12th December 1940 on Great Rhos.***

**Crash site map number 23        Map reference 146/183632**

The prototype Wellington first flew on 15th June 1936, although the first production aircraft did not make its initial flight until eighteen months later. No doubt the crash of the prototype (K4049) had some impact on the production programme.

The first Wellingtons had Vickers gun turrets in nose and tail (L4230 was one of these) but after the initial batch of one hundred and eighty machines had been produced the more efficient Frazer-Nash turrets were fitted.

Powered by two Bristol Pegasus XVlll engines of 1,000 hp each, the Wellington could achieve a maximum speed of 235 mph and was the mainstay of Bomber Command in the early war years.

On 18th December 1939, twenty four Wellington Mk 1s attempted an armed reconnaissance of the Wilhelmshaven area. Intercepted by Bf 109 and Bf 110 fighters of the Luftwaffe, ten Wellingtons were shot down without a bomb being dropped. Shortly after, the Wellington was relegated to the night bomber role, where, under the cover of darkness, they operated until October 1943.

The Ridgeway is one of the oldest green roads in Britain and crosses the Berkshire Downs, eventually leading to the ancient sites of Avebury and beyond.

At the base of the Downs, to the north, stands Harwell airfield. The runways can still be seen, as can many barrack blocks and hangars. (No longer in use for flying, it is, at the time of writing, the home of the UK Atomic Energy Authority.) This airfield was opened in 1937 during the pre-war expansion period and, as part of 12 Group, was an OTU for most of the war. 15 OTU, a main Wellington training unit, suffered more than its fair share of crashes and had the dubious distinction of providing one of the few Mark 1 Wellingtons to crash in Wales (L4256 crashed on the day prior to the subject of this chapter).

On 12th December 1940, Wellington Mk 1 L4230 of 'A' Flight took off on a training flight to Aberaeron, on the coast of Cardigan Bay.

The crew:

| | |
|---|---|
| Squadron Leader G. LEARNER, | Screen Pilot |
| Sergeant EARL, | Pilot |
| Sergeant J DOULL, | W/Op |
| Sergeant T MORLEY, | Navigator |
| Sergeant MARTIN, | Air Gunner |
| Sergeant MULLIN, | Air Gunner |

Whilst over the Radnor hills, with Sergeant Earl at the controls, the damp December air caused severe icing and the starboard engine (No 1611446) stopped. In the thick mist, Sgt Earl, despite only nineteen hours solo on type but with great skill and perhaps an equal amount of luck, pulled off a wheels-up landing on the plateau of Great Rhos, 2166 feet, all crew members stepping out of the wreckage uninjured!

Sgts Earl and Morley set off through the mist, coming down into New Radnor village. Three hours later they returned to bring down the remaining crew and were all soon tucking into a good meal and, most likely, a few pints in the village pub.

Much of the aircraft was salvaged by the RAF and it is rumoured that some wreckage, not immediately removed, was brought down by the owner of the pub, with a tractor and trailer. The remains were then set on fire. Whether this was done at the time or later in the war, to avoid it being reported as a 'new'

**The crash site on Great Rhos with fragments in the foreground.**

crash, is not clear.

From Haines Mill, on the A44, the walk up Great Rhos is by a clearly defined footpath which rises quite steeply but involves no rock climbing. The path, indeed, passes through the site itself but eyes must be kept firmly on the heather to avoid missing it altogether. Considering that nearly sixty years have passed and that thousands of walkers must have traversed this path, it is surprising that anything at all remains. There are, however, many small fragments and solidified pools of alloy still to be seen, testifying to the ability and good fortune of Sgt Earl on that chill December day.

Some of the crashes described in this book can be read about in other publications and I, of course, have read most of them. However, I discovered early on not to take everything I read as gospel; many of the map references are wrong, the initial source being in error, and aircraft numbers and crew members incorrectly recorded.

I now check for myself any important details and, of course, visit each site personally, which is the whole point of this book.

It was, therefore, with no little interest that my researches at the RAF Museum unearthed an intriguing discrepancy. The Form 1180 crash records show that the screen pilot was not, in fact,

Squadron Leader LEARNER but a Sergeant LEATHER.

It is true that I had wondered why a Squadron Leader should be on the aircraft on a routine training flight and this seemed to justify my doubts.

Wishing to know more of Sergeant Leather, I contacted the Ministry of Defence Personnel Centre only to discover that, despite the name on the F1180, no such Sergeant Leather existed!

Ah well – maybe the others were right after all. Perhaps Squadron Leader Learner was on board and even at the controls, accounting for the skilful aircraft handling.

I decided to find out more about the Squadron Leader and, again, enlisted the help of the MoD. Imagine my surprise to be told that there was no Squadron Leader Learner pilot during the war, in fact only one other Learner of that rank and he was in a ground branch. I then decided to try to trace Sergeant Earl, admittedly an unpromising task after all the intervening years. I discovered that he had been commissioned and had, indeed, survived the war. The MoD have proved helpful by forwarding a letter to his last known address but, unfortunately, all my attempts to find him have been to no avail.

So who was flying L4230 on 12th December 1940? I would put my money on Sergeant Earl but then, who was Squadron Leader Geoffrey Learner? Did he really exist and, if so, why doesn't the MoD know of him?

**Molten alloy containing steel parts of the aircraft structure.**

***Martinet Mk1 HN888, 595 Squadron, on a transit flight from Pembrey, crashed 22nd December 1946 on Cwm Bach.***

**Crash site map number 24　　　Map reference 148/178647**

In the early war years target towing was carried out by obsolescent types and aircraft such as the Hawker Henley, deemed unsuitable for front-line service. Though a seemingly mundane task, target towing placed stresses on aircraft and more particularly engines, for which they were never designed. Thus about twenty five per cent of Henleys crashed as a result of engine related failures.

As production of the Master advanced trainer was coming to an end at its Woodley factory, Miles Aircraft designed the Martinet as a target tug from the outset, utilising many components from the Master. Mainly of wooden construction, it was powered by a nine cylinder Bristol Mercury 870 hp radial engine (special attention being paid to the cooling system). This gave it a top speed of some 240 mph. Stowage was provided for six drogue targets and the winch could be either electrically operated or wind driven from a pylon mounted on the port side of the fuselage. By the time production ceased, in 1945, some 1700 aircraft had been built and it equipped fifteen squadrons, continuing in service for some years after the end of hostilities.

HN888 was one of the first batch of machines built by Phillips and Powis (Miles Aircraft Ltd) at its Reading factory. Powered by a Mercury XXX, serial number 101682, it belonged to 595

**Looking down Cwm Bach from the crash site. The engine is near the stream below.**

squadron of 11 Group Fighter Command, based at Pembrey.

With Christmas 1945 fast approaching, Flt Lt R Howard and his colleague Flying Officer M Davies sought authorisation to fly to Castle Bromwich, near to where they planned to spend their leave. The Flight Commander failed to check the pilots' flight plan and to give instructions on procedures to be adopted in the event of bad weather. Squadron standing orders made it clear that pilots should return to base when heavy cloud was encountered but this may have related to target-towing duties rather than transit flights.

Despite a poor weather forecast the pair decided to take-off, though which of them was at the controls is not known. The last message received put them over the Brecon Beacons but, shortly after, the aircraft entered cloud and crashed into the steep hillside at Cwm Bach killing both occupants.

Castle Bromwich is to the north-east of Brecon, whereas Cwm Bach, leading up to Great Rhos, lies in a south-easterly direction. There is, therefore, a possibility that the crew of HN888 had decided to turn back at this point, but this cannot be established.

When the aircraft was reported overdue, four Spitfires searched the area but to no avail. Further fruitless searches were made on December 22nd, 23rd, 24th and 26th. (On December 30th a party sent out to investigate a report of wreckage near Aberystwyth found this to be a previously reported but unconnected crash.) On 2nd February 1946, forty three days after being reported missing, the police sent a message to RAF Aberporth stating that a shepherd had found the wreckage of an aircraft in the hills not far from New Radnor. A search party on 3rd February confirmed this as the missing Martinet; the crew were still in the cockpit, their bodies preserved by the sub-zero temperatures.

After visiting the site of Wellington L4230, at Great Rhos, it is but a mile or so to the steep slope of Cwm Bach where HN888 met its fate. Only small fragments remain but down at the bottom of the valley lies the Mercury engine. Despite resolute attempts by the Abergavenny ATC, it still stubbornly resists recovery.

***Harvard 1 N7077, No. 10 Flying Training School, on a practice flight, crashed 18th November 1939 at Tyn a Dol Farm.***

**Crash site map number 25** **Map reference 136/903802**

Manufactured by North American Aviation at Inglewood, California, the Harvard was one of the first American aircraft purchased by the RAF. The first order in June 1938, for two hundred aircraft, was completed one year later. In total, over five thousand Harvards were delivered to the RAF and Commonwealth air forces.

No 3 Flying Training School at Grantham took delivery of the first aircraft in December 1938 and the Harvard remained in service, as an advanced trainer, until 1955. A number of Harvards were still in use at the experimental establishment at Boscombe Down, Wiltshire, into the 1970s, where they were used as photographic chase aircraft during air dropping trials.

Powered by a Pratt and Whitney Wasp R1340 radial engine of 550 hp, the Harvard could attain a maximum speed of 205 mph. The most prominent feature of the Harvard, however, was its sound. The direct drive propeller resulted in high tip speeds giving it a shrill, rasping note, once heard never forgotten.

**The first Harvard delivered to the RAF. The one that crashed near the A44 was of this batch.**

There are probably hundreds of Harvards surviving today in the hands of aviation enthusiasts. Anyone who has watched films such as 'Tora, Tora, Tora' will have seen them, (painted white and with fur-helmeted, evil-looking oriental pilots) masquerading as the famous Zero fighter, to which they bear a passing resemblance – once rounded wing tips have been added along with tapering of the cockpit cover.

N7077 was one of the first order of Harvards. It was allocated to No 1 FTS in May 1939 before being sent to No 10 Service FTS, at Ternhill Shropshire, in October of the same year. (The first Harvard serial number was N7000)

745512 Sgt J W R Parr joined the RAF Volunteer Reserve before the outbreak of war, receiving his initial training on Tiger Moth biplanes at No 15 Elementary and Reserve FTS, Redhill Surrey. There he clocked up twenty six hours dual and thirty two hours solo flying, before being posted to No 10 FTS, at Ternhill, for advanced training on Harvards.

After five hours dual he went solo and shortly after, on 18th November 1939, was detailed for a solo flight in N7077. The exercise was to practise medium rate turns, take-offs and landings; the proverbial 'circuits and bumps'.

During these manoevres he strayed, whether intentionally or not is unknown, about sixty miles to the south-west of his base. Weather conditions had deteriorated and visibility was down to just over a mile when he descended into the gloom, finding himself only about thirty feet above the ground. In making a sharp turn to avoid the hillside, the aircraft stalled, crashing into a field alongside the railway embankment at Llangurig. Sergeant Parr was severely injured. The railway embankment, which ends at the crash site, was part of an ambitious plan to join Manchester to Milford Haven by rail. Building the next part of the line would have needed an Isambard Kingdom Brunel, in addition to a multi-millionaire. Neither being available, only one passenger train ran to Llangurig and that was in 1861.

Little or nothing has been written about this crash, so I decided on a visit to Llangurig to knock on local doors. Few people had any recollection of the event, none being able to pinpoint the site. Before giving up, I decided to put up a notice in

**The crash site of N7077 is opposite the farm buildings where the field is flooded.**

the local Post Office and, not long after, was rewarded with a call from Mrs Joyce Tannat. She saw the crash remains at the time, could tell me exactly where it happened and it was her father who helped to free the pilot from the wreckage.

Joe Manley, her father, rode his bicycle down to the field where the Harvard crashed and, together with Trevor Jones from the garage nearby, lifted the pilot to the roadside. His condition was serious and, as no ambulance was available, they flagged down a passing van. Joe rolled up his jacket, an old policeman's coat, put it under the injured airman's head and tried to make him comfortable. Unfortunately, by the time they arrived at Llanidloes hospital Sgt Parr was dead.

Joyce Tannat told me that she saw the aircraft circling for some time before the crash but, oddly enough, remembers it as a clear, not cloudy day. This might be a trick of memory for surely, if it was a clear day, the pilot would have climbed and soon realised where he was. He could, perhaps, have been engaged in unauthorised low flying but there is no evidence of this.

Joyce went to see the aircraft later that day. On the following day she trooped down to look at it again with fellow pupils of Llangurig school, although it was under RAF guard by then. The wreckage was not taken away for several days and provided much interest for the local people.

It is most likely that the aircraft was dismantled rather than broken up, thus leaving little or nothing at the site.

The subsequent Court of Inquiry stated that the pilot was off course owing to bad weather conditions and was trying to fix his position. Because of inexperience, he lost control during a turn and stalled in from twenty five to thirty feet AGL. The aircraft was at first classified as Repairable but this was later changed to Written Off. An examination of the aircraft could find no defect in either engine or airframe.

The site is alongside the A44, just across the road from Tyn a Dol farm. After gaining permission, I made a thorough search of the area but could find no evidence of the crash. As the aircraft appears to have been removed almost intact there can be little hope of finding anything. Recovery must have posed few problems for the salvage team as their task lay only a few hundred yards from the main road.

***Hunter F4 XE680, 738 Squadron, on a ground attack exercise from Brawdy, crashed 3rd March 1969 near Dolhelfa.***

**Crash site map number 26　　　Map reference 136/929738**

The Hawker Hunter, many might say, was the last of the really beautiful fighter aircraft. Coming from the same stable as the incomparable pre-war Fury, it epitomised the old aviation axiom, 'If it looks right, it is right'. Since the Hunter's departure. the fighter aircraft has become more aggressive and missile-like in appearance; functional, but not particularly attractive.

Brawdy, in 1969, was a Royal Naval Air Service establishment and home of 738 squadron. On 3rd March Sub Lt Hugh Mansel-Smith (23) of Surbiton, Surrey, took off in XE680 on an exercise to make a simulated attack on a target near Rhayader. On reaching the general area, however, Sub Lieutenant Mansel-Smith found the valley shrouded in mist and low cloud, which resulted in his overshooting the target. People in nearby Rhayader were reported to have said that the aircraft narrowly missed the local church tower. Mr J A Thomas told a reporter from the Brecon and Radnor Express that, when he saw the aircraft, it was upside down.

On making his second attempt, the pilot, realising that he was heading for the hillside in an almost vertical bank and would be unable to pull out in time, used his ejection seat to abandon the aircraft. XE680 crashed alongside the main A44 road and exploded. Witnesses at the time reported seeing flaming debris thrown one hundred feet into the air.

The pilot, having ejected with the aircraft on its side, had insufficient time to separate from the seat and was killed instantly. Traffic on the road was trapped by blazing wreckage; Lyn Foster of Rhayader and an ambulance with two patients on board were unable to proceed until the arrival of the emergency services.

Later, Lt Cdr William Peppe of RNAS Brawdy confirmed that

**The A44 road is closed awaiting the arrival of the emergency services. Part of the wreckage can be seen on the extreme right.**

The tail of X680 can be seen with its Brawdy marking 'BY' on the fin.
The same scene today. A sheep stands where the tail of XE680 came to rest.

the pilot had crashed, during a second attempt to complete his mission in deteriorating weather conditions.

In 1992, whilst collecting material for my first book and when looking for the site of Defiant T4008, the farmer had told me of the Hunter crash but I was unable to find any evidence of it. This time, however, I was to strike lucky. A local historian, Mr C V Davies from Llanidloes, had read the book and offered to describe the scene to me. On examining photographs he took at the time, I realised quite clearly that I had been searching some distance from the actual crash site.

Returning once more, I found a number of tiny fragments: a single turbine blade looking as though it had only just left the factory, a piece of plastic material from the nose-cone, still with light grey external paint adhering to it, but little else.

The actual site has, nevertheless, been pinpointed and recorded at last.

**A turbine blade and a fragment of the nose showing the grey and white paint.**

***Hunter F6 XJ637, No1 Tactical Weapons Unit, on a navigational training flight from Brawdy, crashed 14th March 1979 at Felindre Isaf Farm.***

**Crash site map number 27** **Map reference 146/551558**

By 1979 Brawdy had become No 1 Tactical Weapons Unit, RAF. Two of the aircraft on strength were XJ635 and the subject of this section, XJ637. Both crashed in Wales within fifteen miles of each other.

On 14th March 1979, XJ637 was on a navigational training flight when, crossing the coast south of Aberystwyth in an easterly direction, the engine stopped. At low altitude there was no time for the pilot to re-start the engine, so he ejected. Landing in a forest nearby he found himself suspended by his parachute in the trees, cut himself free with his emergency knife (strapped to his leg) and climbed down, little the worse for his experience. The aircraft hit the ground and exploded. The main part of the fuselage landed near Felindre Isaf, then farmed by Mrs Anne Reynolds. Fire appliances rushed from nearby Lampeter and a helicopter from Brawdy, while curious sightseers were kept away

**XJ637 crashed in the foreground, whilst the pilot landed in the trees behind.**

by police for fear of live ammunition in the wreckage exploding.

Mr D Wright, present owner of the land, saw the aircraft from his farm, Talfan, which overlooks the Aeron Vale. He watched the pilot parachute to safety and was, therefore, able to give me the exact position of the crash at first-hand.

A short search, nevertheless, revealed nothing, though, as is often the case, further visits may well unearth fragments which have been overlooked

The name of the pilot is not given here, as Government regulations prohibit the release of information for thirty years. However, when a crew member is killed there must be an inquest and the names of those involved made public.

Within a twenty mile radius of Devil's Bridge there are five Hunter crash sites: those of XJ635, XJ637, XL575, XE680 and, finally, XE649. (The precise location of the latter has yet to be recorded.)

**Last of the good-lookers: Prototype Hunter.**

**A Hunter of the famous Black Arrows Aerobatic Team.**

# ACKNOWLEDGEMENTS

The author wishes to acknowledge the following individuals and organisations for their invaluable help and guidance and especially for providing photographic and documentary material. (Every effort has been made to locate the owners of material, origins of which are unknown.)

*Aeroplane Monthly*, British Aerospace, Battle of Britain Memorial Flight, Hugh Cawdron, R Cooling, Clwyd Record Office, Harry Davies, Rob Evans, Sara Furse, Flintshire Council, J Gerrard, Roger Hampson, Alex Henshaw, John Hughes, Imperial War Museum, Mrs Mackeson – Sandbach, Mirror Group Newspapers, Ministry of Defence, Anna McIlwaine, Public Record Office, RAF Museum, Rolls-Royce plc, Matthew Rimmer, Hedley Richards, Len Roberts, South African Air Force, USAF, Idwal Vaughan and especially Shirley Evans.

**The body of an airman was found 2nd March 1945 in Wales.**
**"Known Unto God"**

# INDEX

# Aviation Ghosts

by Kevin Desmond

Do you believe in ghosts?' is a question more likely than not to provoke an emphatic yes or no answer. This book challenges disbelievers to reassess their position. Intrigued that so many airstations, some with household names such as Lindholme, Cardington and Hendon, lay in a straight line bearing South by South East 165 degress, Kevin Desmond decided to investigate further. His ensuing journey described in this book, more than justified his curiosity and unearthed a disturbing number of seemingly inexplicable incidents. A book to fascinate not just aviation and paranormal specialists but to the general reader.

ISBN: 0-85052-620-5 224pp Hardback £16.95

## Dark Peak Aircraft Wrecks 1
## Dark Peak Aircraft Wrecks 2

*Ron Collier & Roni Wilkinson*

These two handy pocket-size volumes tell the story of aviation this century through the remains of aircraft still to be found in the Peak District National Park. Over 50 aircraft from biplanes to modern jets have come to grief on the Pennines: Training Command, Bomber Command, Fighter Command, the USAAF and USN are all represented in the remains on the local high ground. Map references, along with the background stories, are all included in these highly popular guides aimed at at fell walkers and aviation enthusiasts. Both books are heavily illustrated.

**VOLUME 1**: 160 pages **£9.95** paperback ISBN: 0-85052-457-1
**VOLUME 2**: 192 pages **£9.95** paperback ISBN: 0-85052-336-2